WORLD WAR II

WORLD WAR II

From the Battle Front to the Home Front

Arkansans Tell Their Stories

Edited by Kay B. Hall

THE UNIVERSITY OF ARKANSAS PRESS
FAYETTEVILLE   1995

99 98 97 96 95   5 4 3 2 1

Designed by Ellen Beeler

⊗ The paper used in this publication meets the minimum requirements of the American National Standard for Permanence of Paper for Printed Library Materials Z39.48-1984.

Library of Congress Cataloging-in-Publication Data

World War II : from the battle front to the home front, Arkansans tell their
    stories / edited by Kay B. Hall.
        p.   cm.
    ISBN 1-55728-396-6 (alk. paper). — ISBN 1-55728-395-8 (pbk. :
alk. paper)
    1. World War, 1939–1945—Personal narratives, American. 2. World
War, 1939–1945—Arkansas. I. Hall, Kay B.
    D811.A2W618   1995
    940.54'81'73—dc20   95-6845
                                                                  CIP

Contents

Introduction

Library shelves hold numerous accounts of World War II. Documents and photographs cover every aspect of the causes and effects of a war that began in Europe in 1939 and drew us into it in December of 1941. Although the war has been over for fifty years, historians continue to write, revise, or expand earlier accounts. Only names, dates, battles, and casualties remain the same. This book makes no attempt to transform the way people think about World War II, but rather to approach it from a unique direction.

The stories in this book are derived from interviews with current residents of Arkansas and reflect the impact of the war on them as individuals. They view the past from their own perspectives, typifying the ripple effects of those changing times.

While each differs in point of view and circumstance, a common thread runs through all the stories, a thread of selective recall, an ability to dwell on the positive. Looking back from this distance in time has softened some perceptions, dimmed some memories, but everyone shared, as honestly as they could, what they did remember.

Historic accuracy of any period is important, but no less important is understanding the feelings and thoughts of those who lived through it. How people living in Arkansas, an agricultural state in the middle of a neutral country, felt about entering a war being fought on foreign soil is revealing and explains some of what came to follow World War II.

Each person recalls the struggle to recover from the depression years of the 1930s, and this colors perceptions of World War II. Changes brought by the United States entering the war ended the economic slump and brought a new prosperity. It resulted in war and munitions plants, prisoner-of-war camps, Japanese relocation internment camps, and military camps and brought additional government jobs. Residents relocated to all corners of the state, and some even left Arkansas temporarily, to work in other parts of the country or to be with their mates stationed at bases and camps from coast to coast. Housing shortages were widespread.

War casualties were carefully counted on the battlefields and beaches and in the trenches and hospitals. The home front had its own battles to fight and, in its own way, casualties. There was a shortage of goods, and in some cases a shortage of good will. There were still unresolved prejudices toward women and blacks in the workplace. Prejudice in hiring and of co-workers was felt by many who flocked to the factories to fill jobs once held solely by men, sometimes solely by white men.

It has been more than fifty years since the dust settled from World War II. While many rely only on their memories, others kept their own documented accounts in journals, letters, and photos. The memories recorded here paint a portrait of the spirit of the times rather than straight historical fact, humanity rather than cause and effect, even when those memories are fragmented.

For most, looking back was rewarding, revealing a common experience of learning shared with others during a time when almost everyone bore a burden, made sacrifices, willingly shared housing, or felt compassion for others. Some recall with nostalgia, and others remember with horror what they witnessed or survived. But for many, the telling of it was a closure—a resolution of one of the most written-about periods in history.

As a child of World War II, I also looked back and drew on my own memories, surprised at how much I did recall. My parents and I were living in Detroit in December of 1941; I was in the third grade. When I learned about Pearl Harbor, we were in our second-floor apartment, and I heard a newsboy's cry from down on the street for the first time in my life, "Extra, extra, read all about it!" I remember my dad going downstairs to buy a copy of the paper. My aunt and uncle from the apartment across the hall gathered in our living room, and we, like millions of other Americans, all huddled around the radio.

Over the next three and a half years, most of my uncles went off to war. My Uncle Goran, Mother's oldest brother, had served as a marine in World War I. I only recently learned that after that war he was selected as an honor guard at the Tomb of the Unknown Soldier. But for World War II, the marines turned him down as too old. Not to be deterred, he joined the navy and saw some of the worst fighting in the Pacific. Now dead, he was an artist, and he painted the ships at sea and the ports he'd seen in vivid oils and bright watercolors.

My dad, only twenty-eight when World War II started, tried to enlist, but was rejected. The stigma of being 4-F must have hurt him a lot, particularly when his brother was accepted. He tried again when they were taking just about everyone, but they didn't want someone without a thumb on his gun hand, which he had lost in a plant accident.

His brother, Joe, went into the army and, when sent overseas, let my father take over his new car and car payments. I remember it well, a '42 Chevy coupe, one of the last to roll off the Detroit assembly lines for the duration of the war. Auto plants had been quickly converted to war plants.

Despite most of our family working scattered around Detroit and other family back home in southern Illinois where we were all born, we remained a close family.

The war brought us more money than we had ever seen. On payday, Mother and Daddy shopped for groceries at A&P. There was a carton of Pepsi every week, something unheard of during the depression. At one point my father had worked on the WPA (Work Projects Administration; earlier known as Works Progress Administration), and those times weren't forgotten. They weren't discussed, however, and I recall Mother's reticence at talking about those days even after I was grown, as if it were shameful.

Mother's sister, Esther Elizabeth Johnson, joined the Women's Army Auxiliary Corps (WAAC—later shortened to WACS, the Women's Army Corps) at age nineteen. Women for the first time in U.S. history were permitted to join the armed services. Colorful posters made service life seem glamorous, quite different from reality. There were WAVES (Women Appointed for Voluntary Emergency Service in the navy), WAAFS (Women's Auxiliary Air Force), and Spars (members of the Women's Reserve of the Coast Guard). Over two hundred thousand American women served their country in World War II. I remember my aunt looking great in her uniform. She wore her hair in a chignon beneath her army cap.

David Boorstin and Brooks Mather Kelley, in *A History of the United States,* report that in addition to the women in the armed services, another six million women joined the ten million already working outside the home. They could no longer be accused of taking jobs from men with families to support; they were working for the war effort and replacing men who were needed to fight. The only men left at home were either in vital services or too young, too old, or unfit to serve.

Mother's sister in Searcy, Evelyne Russell, like so many young women during the war, lived with her parents in Benton, Illinois, for the duration. Her husband, a career army officer, served in the Pacific. Her late sister, Virginia Self, stayed with her in-laws part of the time while her husband was in the navy. The youngest sister, Mary Ellen Rei, followed her husband throughout the states from army camp to army camp. His unit never went overseas; he guarded prisoners of war in this country.

According to Evelyne, "Everyone walked to work. Most businesses were either on the square—Benton was the county seat—or in the first blocks off the square of North, South, East, and West Main Streets. Pop drove to work in the coal mines, about six miles, but there wasn't any running to the store in the car—no gas and no second cars."

At school, students collected scrap metal, grease, newspapers, grocery bags, and aluminum foil. Meat drippings were used to make glycerin for gunpowder. We bought savings stamps and Liberty bonds—every Tuesday was "stamp day" at school. For ten cents you could buy a stamp; when you had purchased enough for a bond (the smallest cost $18.75), which, in effect, was a loan to the government, you received a bond that could be redeemed in ten years for $25.

Families mailed packages to men and women in uniform. Every time we gave up a luxury, such as on "meatless Tuesday," we felt we were furnishing an essential to the troops for the war effort—a small sacrifice but, nonetheless, a small victory over self-indulgence. World War II made Spam a household word. It was referred to as "ham that hadn't passed its physical."

In town, mail was delivered twice a day, and V-mail, even with most of it censored, was important—just about the most important communication on the home front during the war.

I remember the race riot in Detroit and understanding nothing of what was going on—except that for a short period of time I wasn't permitted to ride the Jefferson streetcar alone or with other young friends.

Saturday movie matinees at the war's beginning were only ten cents (half the usual admission price); by war's end, the luxury tax increased the cost to fourteen cents. A luxury tax was placed on all nonessentials.

Boorstin and Kelley write that Americans were paying the highest federal taxes in history during World War II. At the highest end of the earning scale, an individual could be taxed as much as 94 percent. The high taxes covered only 41 percent of the cost of the war. The rest of the money was borrowed from banks by our government. Inflation was a constant government problem, and despite price freezes the cost of living rose 29 percent. But by the same token, wages increased by 70 percent.

Nylon and silk were used in the manufacture of parachutes, resulting in a silk or nylon hose shortage, and I recall newsreels of women overseas retrieving parachutes and using the fabric, sometimes for wedding dresses. Shoes were rationed (an army marches through lots of boots), and most of my family's shoe coupons went to buy shoes for me. I was hard on shoes.

Daddy and Grandpa had victory gardens, and the women canned. For many that was just life as usual, but all women, even working ones, were encouraged to do their part. According to *Discovering America's Past*, a book published by *Reader's Digest*, troops overseas consumed twenty thousand tons of food every day—that's a lot of victuals. And that's why it was necessary to ration certain food items at home, making it important to grow and can your own foods.

We moved back to southern Illinois when I was in fourth grade. Mother and I traveled on ahead by bus while Daddy stayed behind until he could save enough gas for the six-hundred-mile trip home. Mother rented us a house in West Frankfort. We received a telegram saying that Daddy, while in the car, had been hit by a streetcar on Jefferson Avenue. His trunk had been filled with five-gallon gas cans. Miracles do happen; the gas did not explode. He recovered from the accident, had the car repaired, and eventually joined us.

Grade schools were filled with war posters. Posters, in fact, greeted you everywhere. I recall in particular those proclaiming "Buy War Bonds." Rosie the Riveter was recognized by everyone, and military posters are still as fresh in my memory as if it were yesterday; the nurse with her red-lined cape was quite popular, and the image was that of a fresh-faced lovely young lady—not always the image these poor girls received once recruited and in uniform. Being a nurse to servicemen, and thus a woman of "easy virtue," was just one of the prejudices fought during wartime. Posters, especially movie posters, depicted the Japanese as evil and distorted—caricatures that had squinty-eyed faces with buck teeth. For some reason I've never figured out, most posters had them wearing glasses with thick lenses. Germans fared little better, but the red German flags with the black swastikas captured the imagination of the boys better than the symbol of the rising sun. The boys would draw swastikas on notebooks or walls and get into trouble at school.

Slogans were as plentiful and powerful as the posters—
"Loose Lips Sink Ships"—and the standard excuse for long
delays, out-of-stock items, or slow service was, "There's a
war on, you know."

Kilroy, with his message "Kilroy was here," seemed to be
everywhere. It was nothing more than the drawing of the
top of a head, two eyes, large ears, and a huge proboscis
extending over a straight line representing a wall. How his
image found its way from factory crates to the schoolroom
remains a mystery and anyone's guess.

Cartoon characters went patriotic for the "war effort";
Captain Marvel, Superman, Terry and the Pirates, and even
Dick Tracy were all fighting Nazis to make the world a better place. Films were churned out by Hollywood with sentimental messages, all using liberty, patriotism, and the
heartbreak of separated young lovers as fodder for the
propaganda mill. Songs came to us from across the ocean.
"The White Cliffs of Dover" was only one of many. The
Andrews Sisters made "Don't Sit under the Apple Tree" and
many other memorable songs, with lyrics most of us still
remember.

Windows were filled with small banners with blue stars
representing husbands, sons, or brothers serving their country. If a gold star was displayed, you knew its meaning—that
family had lost someone in the war. An organization was
later formed for these gold-star mothers and widows.

It was politically correct to hate the Japanese, of course.
Tojo and Hirohito photos made good dartboards for many
children; the faces were as well known as those of Hitler and
Mussolini. Even comic book characters changed to reflect
the times. The Green Hornet's faithful Japanese servant,
Cato, became a Filipino.

Our government rounded up Japanese Americans, many

born here in the United States, and placed them in internment camps called relocation centers. Two camps were at Jerome and Rohwer. Families were forced to leave their homes and businesses without recompense.

Blacks risked their lives for their country, also. No job was too dirty or too dangerous for them, yet it would take another war before they were permitted to bunk and shower with whites.

Cigarettes were in short supply and were used for barter overseas. There were reports of black markets at home and abroad. Popular brands, such as Lucky Strikes, Camels, and Chesterfields, were scarce stateside, but an off brand, Wings, was available for ten cents a pack and had a little card with an airplane on it in each pack. Those cards were traded much like baseball cards and would probably be valuable today.

Gas rationing gave the average ration book holder four gallons a week. But farmers were given additional gas, and those holding critical jobs—priests and pastors, doctors—all received extra rations. I don't remember any gripes or squabbles at the "filling stations" (the popular name at the time). I do recall hearing that while the average person had barely enough gas to get by, the fat cats in Washington got all they wanted. I didn't understand that until I later read that congressmen had voted to give themselves an "X" sticker, which allowed them to buy unlimited amounts of gasoline.

By war's end, rubber was still in short supply. I recall films and documentaries on the development of a product that was "rubberlike." Nothing, however, replaced rubber for tires, and even bike tires were difficult to find during the war. I remember growing up thinking it was commonplace to have frequent flat tires. It seems Daddy was always helping someone change a tire or patch an inner tube.

Processed foods required rationing stamps. Meat, fats, oil, coffee, sugar, and even heating fuel were all rationed. Heating-fuel allowances were based on the square footage of the floor plan.

The seeds of World War II were planted after World War I when the Treaty of Versailles was signed. Its provisions caused much bitterness in Germany, but even Italy, an ally during World War I, resented not receiving a bigger share of the spoils of war. It was just the right climate for dictators to rise from among the common people to champion a cause. Asia, also, was a place of unrest. As early as 1931, Japan had invaded Manchuria. The Japanese had learned the lessons of imperialism from the West and wanted Manchuria for a clear path to mainland China. Russia saw the danger in Japan being able to march through China to get to them.

Arkansas, a small agricultural state, can be forgiven for not having seen the war coming. It lay in the center of a safe, neutral country, feeling virtually impregnable. The fighting was across two oceans, not so close then as technology has made it today.

Arkansas couldn't possibly have seen what a large part it would come to play in American and world history, what a giant of the poultry and trucking industry it would become, or how valuable its resources would be. Modern technology and automation have attracted world trade, and Arkansas has been more visible to the world and to the rest of the United States since World War II.

The stories in this book will bear witness to the will and ability that the people in Arkansas have to survive and recover from the many changes they have undergone because of the depression and World War II. The war brought Arkansas into a new era, and once the war was over, the state's emphasis shifted from the war effort to a higher standard of living and to higher education. Arkansas has become a leader in transportation, commerce, communication, and electronic technology and in research and development in the agricultural programs at the University of Arkansas.

Alfred E. West

I F THE SURPRISE Japanese attack on Pearl Harbor on the morning of December 7, 1941, had come just a few minutes after eight o'clock, Alfred E. West and many of his shipmates would have been ashore on liberty. But the attacking aircraft arrived a few minutes before eight, and as a result, West became an eyewitness to one of this country's most humiliating disasters.

West, who now lives at Hindsville in Madison County, is a native of Indiana. He enlisted in the navy in June 1940, and arrived at Pearl Harbor in early December 1941. As a nineteen-year-old seaman, first class, he was assigned to the command ship of the Base Force Fleet, the *Argonne,* a former World War I troopship that had been converted for use by the commander of the base's fleet of ships and tugs into a sort of floating office.

The *Argonne* was tied to the "Ten-Ten" dock. The battleship USS *Pennsylvania,* which carried the flag of the commander of the Pacific Fleet, was in dry dock elsewhere or it would have been directly across from the *Argonne.* In its place were the *Ogallala* and a cruiser, the *Helena,* to the best of West's recollection; in the attack, both ships were hit and turned on their sides. The focus of the Japanese attack, Ford

Island, around which battleships and carriers docked, was within sight of the *Argonne.*

"I had just finished dressing to go ashore—I had my neckerchief on and everything, but we couldn't leave the ship until the quartermaster sounded eight o'clock," West said of that historic morning. "It was probably five minutes before eight when we heard the noise of the bombs exploding on Ford Island. They were bombing it to begin with because we had planes there."

West asked a marine sergeant what was happening and was told that the Japanese were attacking. He wasn't convinced until he looked out of a porthole and saw fire and smoke boiling up from Ford Island. "Even then, I didn't believe it. I didn't want to. I was just in shock—I guess everybody was. Within two or three minutes they sounded general quarters. That means everybody to your battle stations. Mine was passing out ammunition." West and a partner carried heavy boxes of ammunition from the magazine compartment up onto the deck, supplying the .50-caliber and .30-caliber machine guns as well as a few three-inch pedestal-mounted guns. Finally, they were told to stop "because we'd reached the point of saturation—we had so much ammunition up there they couldn't move." With no ammunition to haul, West found himself a spectator to the attack.

"This may sound a little bit ludicrous, but we watched it from then on, at the lifelines. That was all we could do, just stay out of the way. The Japanese knew exactly where everything was, and they knew that the *Argonne* was no threat to them. The only time I really worried about it was when the second wave of bombers came in.

"There was a formation of bombers at high altitude coming over in V formation, and it was so clear you could see the bombs coming out, coming down in V formation. That's what scared me: I had no idea where they were going to land. If they were off target, they could have hit us just as easy because it was just a matter of a few hundred yards from where we were to the battleships, which is what they were after."

The attack lasted two hours, and witnesses could clearly see the Japanese symbol, the red disk, on the attacking planes' sides and wings. At one point, West recalled, the *Nevada*, which had taken several hits, attempted to get under way but was stopped by orders from an admiral, lest it sink and block the harbor's entrance, trapping the rest of the fleet.

"The attack seemed to go on for so long that I thought we would probably be invaded," said West, adding that he feared they would all be taken prisoners of war. When the attack ended, he volunteered to join the boat crews that began picking up the wounded and taking them to the "Ten-Ten" dock where commandeered civilian vehicles were providing transport to hospitals. West rescued survivors of the *Arizona*, which was in the process of sinking, and the *Nevada*. Many of them were badly burned.

"Then they found out that the underwater net, or anti-submarine screen, which was stretched across the mouth of the harbor, had been broken and that there were minisubs out there; they'd actually sighted them. So we got the order to hunt submarines." This was done by dragging grapnel hooks on heavy lines behind motor launches. Some subs were caught this way.

West left Pearl Harbor a month later to attend the navy's photographic school in Pensacola, Florida, the beginning of a twenty-year naval career. He spent his remaining Pearl Harbor days in work details provisioning ships. His subsequent naval tours during the war sent him to both the

Atlantic and Pacific. After the war, he saw duty at the North Pole, in Korea, and in Japan. "I have to say, honestly, I wasn't bitter, because I felt we did it to ourselves. With all of the information that's come out since the war, I feel that we contributed to our own problems. It was like two children out there scrapping and finally one of them gets hurt. And you must realize that you brought it on yourself."

Harold Falls

HAROLD FALLS SPENT the war years in Wynne, the county seat of Cross County, then just a tiny town of four thousand (Falls eventually served as mayor of Wynne from 1946 to 1971). But they were lonely years for Falls because all his friends were away in the service.

"I'd had polio as a baby, and I was classified 4-F. I was just out of college, and with almost all my friends away, I was pulled into service with several boards and civic projects for Wynne."

One of the boards he served on was the Office of Price Administration (OPA). "I was chairman of the board, and when it came to regulating prices, the situation could get dicey." By dicey, he meant that some businesses became unhappy with the controls, but for the most part, business people cooperated with little grumbling.

"We had to supervise all retail pricing, from farm equipment to groceries. The whole point was to put a ban on price escalation and prevent a black market from flourishing. We didn't want a black market to provide services and supply goods, so we did what we had to do." Merchants were all required to post prices, and one of the OPA board members would monitor and approve the merchants' actions.

"Oh, there were some scalawags and opportunists, but we still had a lot of local town support. In those days we were pretty much dominated by agriculture, the backbone of our economy. Cotton was king as I grew up, and rice was just coming in at the time. We did use the oppressed—cheap labor—a matter of history now."

His family was in the farm machinery equipment business. "When the war started, we were still trying to run the mules off the farm in order to sell our equipment. Then, machinery and tires were at a premium and in short supply. I remember we had a big old combine on display. There was little call for that combine, but one day a man stopped by and offered to buy it. He wasn't a farmer, and I asked him why he wanted it. He said he would buy it just for the tires. They wouldn't have been easy to convert for use, but I didn't sell it to him.

"We had a German POW camp here, and we used the prisoners to clear land for the rice fields just going in. It had to be hand cleared, and the Germans did most of the work. They were kept at our county fairgrounds where we had a lot of primitive buildings. They put up some more, built a stockade fence, and kept the prisoners there. They were a good bunch, as I recall. They were good workers, took a lot of pride in their work. I remember I was out there one day watching a crew of them. They were left to themselves (I don't believe any of them ever tried to escape), and they'd finished clearing. But when the guards got back to them, they were doing drills and marches. They really had a good deal of pride—a little arrogance, too—but we got along with them."

Falls said he even heard from one POW after the war, but without a return address, he couldn't keep in touch.

Rationing was a common part of life then, too. And he

heard a lot about applications made for special allocations. He didn't have much to do with their approval, however.

  " "I know industry and agriculture could apply for and receive supplemental ration cards or allocations that gave them more gasoline or commodities used in special businesses or services, but the rest of us had the standard 'A' cards, basic cards with the regular ration of commodities. Sugar, gas, shoes, meat—several things were in demand and in short supply."

Falls lived at home with his parents and worked in his parents' farm equipment business since his civic work was all on a voluntary basis and unpaid. He had a sister at home who taught school and a brother who served in the navy. They were a pretty typical family, he thought.

Falls still owns his family's farm equipment business, and he has watched Arkansas farmers go from using mules to the latest farm equipment and technology. But when his family first moved from Dardanelle to Wynne, during the worst part of the depression, farmers were going through a very difficult time. And by the time he went into the business at the height of the war, farm machinery businesses and farms were suffering from shortages of labor and equipment.

"A lot of the cheap labor in the state went to places like Detroit and Flint, Michigan, to work in war plants. Some of them never returned. I know some farms used prisoners of war to help farm—they replaced the cheap labor."

When Falls looks back at sitting out the war, he thinks of it as a dark time for him. He felt very much alone except when friends came home on leave. But he served his country and state to the best of his ability, and after the war, his friends came home, elected him mayor, and kept electing him for twenty-five years.

Ray Kellam

FROM THE SPRING of 1942 until his liberation in 1945, U.S. Army Air Corps T.Sgt. Ray A. Kellam was held prisoner of war by the Japanese.

Kellam arrived by ship in May of 1940 at Manila in the Philippines. By 1941, he was helping unload equipment at island air bases. Newer aircraft began arriving to replace old P-26s and Republic P-35s. The new planes should have indicated something was brewing in the Pacific, but on December 5, when the men left work at the Far East Air Force (headquartered at Nielson Field near Manila), they had no idea Pearl Harbor would be bombed before their return on Monday morning.

The first reports of the attack weren't believed, but once confirmed, the airfields awaited orders to bomb Formosa. Word didn't come, however, and Japanese planes from Formosa hit first, bombing both Clark Field and the field at Iba, destroying eighteen B-17s, fifty-three P-40s, and twenty-five other aircraft.

Kellam and the other men cut bamboo stalks to hide the remaining planes, but the C-39 in which he'd made his first military flight was destroyed at Nielson Field. "It burst into flames so hot that even the propellers were melted."

By Christmas Eve, a force of several thousand Japanese had landed at Lanon Bay, southeast of Manila. Gen. Douglas MacArthur and his staff moved to Corregidor, and Manila began its evacuation. All supplies that could be carried were transported to Bataan; the rest were destroyed. Arriving on Bataan was "spooky" with all the sounds of the animals in the jungle: wild pigs, chickens, jungle birds, and monkeys. By January 5, military forces on Bataan were put on half-rations; the only fresh meat came from water buffalo or the horses and mules kept by the cavalry. Rumors of the war and what was happening were rampant. Near January's end, Ray Kellam and some of his outfit went to Quinauan Point and took up positions against six hundred Japanese who had landed.

By March of 1942, General MacArthur had left the Philippines, and Bataan was losing the battle of hunger and disease. "Malaria was widespread and diarrhea, dysentery, and scurvy began to take a toll. I was remarkably healthy, having only an occasional touch of diarrhea and a bout with dengue fever."

Kellam could see Corregidor from his gun position and observed Japanese aircraft bombing the islands. Night raids were commonplace and looked like a spectacular display of deadly fireworks on the horizon.

The ground shook one night, and Kellam wondered what kind of bombs had produced that effect. "Being from the Ozarks, I hadn't experienced an earthquake. I had just experienced my first."

On April 8, 1942, he was called to a meeting on top of the ridge to hear from General King that morning about the surrender. The men were told they could assemble at the airfield at Mariveles. King said they weren't ordered to surrender but instead were told to use their own judgment.

"Most men did go to the airfield, but some moved along the ridge to the north hoping to evade the Japanese by hiding out in the mountains. Dinty Moore, my friend from Oklahoma, and I decided we'd try to get a boat and make it to Australia. We hid out that first night in a cave. We searched and searched in vain for a boat." Finally, they simply took a fishing boat from three Filipinos who accompanied them so they could get their boat back, and they headed out. The only direction open to them was Corregidor, not Australia. After seven hours of paddling, they approached shore. Exhausted, Kellam and Moore sent the Filipinos on their way with their boat and stacked their rifles and slept through the night. Upon awaking, Kellam found that an old rifle had replaced his new one. "During the night, a marine exchanged rifles with me." He accepted this misfortune as another aspect of war.

Bombardment went on unabated through May 5 when Japanese forces landed on the north point of the island. Kellam and his friend had joined some marines on the island who had machine guns and ammunition. The Japanese continued to divebomb them, and the marines were ordered to destroy all arms and ammunition. At the surrender of Corregidor, the men were told to stay at headquarters until further notice from their captors. Space was limited, but any American who wandered away from his outfit was promptly shot by the Japanese. The Japanese distributed some food to the hungry men, but there was no orderly or equitable distribution. Eventually, Kellam and the others were loaded onto boats and sent to Manila. It was a humiliating experience when the Japanese paraded them through the streets to exhibit them as a symbol of their victory over the Americans. Manila wasn't their final destination, however; when they left, they were crammed into small boxcars with only enough room for them to stand. The time in the boxcars was unbearable. The dysentery was uncontrollable, and the prisoners were reduced to an animal state, "each only interested in his own existence for another hour."

Their ride ended at a schoolyard at Cabanatuan, but only for one night. The men were marched without food and water to a prison camp. Those who attempted to drink from the roadside puddles were clubbed. Upon arrival at the camp, the POWs were divided into groups and then into squads of ten. They were told that if one of their squad escaped, the other nine would be shot. If anyone was shot, however, Kellam never knew about it. The men dug latrines, away from their sleeping quarters. They established a kitchen, but the only food was rice and an occasional watery soup in which vegetables had been cooked. "Scurvy, beri-beri, anemia, sore mouths, bleeding gums, pellagra, and other sicknesses were awful. I'd say at least two thousand died that first month. It was impossible to get an accurate count."

By October, Kellam and some other prisoners were transferred to Japan. They were marched back to Cabanatuan and boarded a Japanese transport, the *Totori Maru,* along with Japanese troops.

At Formosa, the prisoners were permitted to bathe with fresh water from hoses. They reached their destination, Osaka, in November 1942. Some of them were sent to other destinations. Kellam was sent to Tokyo by electric train and then to Kawasaki. "I remember," he said, his voice revealing the irony, "it was November 11, 1942, our Armistice Day."

The hardest adjustment for most of the men was the poor diet. The topic of food was a constant one and an obsession for many of the men. "We couldn't seem to help ourselves. We'd prepare menus in our heads and talk about how we'd prepare meals. But once our B-29s started bombing Japan, we were back to just trying to stay alive."

Kellam and other POWs were moved from one site to another to augment the work force in manufacturing plants and to do heavy labor. They worked alongside other POWs from Korea and China. "Dysentery continued to be a problem, and on the walk to and from work, the men would run frequently to both sides of the road." There were two work groups, the Sokos and the Jokos. The Sokos had to remove flaws from steel bars with grinding wheels. The Jokos were given air-operated tools with chisels. Kellam said he looked around "the whole portrait in grime and wondered how a clean kid from the Ozark hills could wind up in a place like this."

He soon graduated to working on the railroad, a better job because he could breathe fresh air, but the labor was hard and the hours long. While prisoners of war in America were making several dollars a day, in Japan POWs received ten cents a day and were paid infrequently. Sometimes they could bribe a guard to bring them extra food with the money they earned.

While the other men continued to succumb to dysentery, Kellam seemed to thrive on the Japanese food. He was determined to learn to survive on it. If the Japanese could survive on it, he reasoned, so could he. He weighed between 150 and 160 pounds when captured. By the time of his release, he was down to 110. "But I was in pretty good shape physically. All that work on the railroad toughened me up."

It wasn't long until the prisoners began to hear about a new camp under construction. Some of the men were scheduled to be moved again, and Kellam was one of them. "We were sent to Dispatch Number 5 [a prison camp] with the marines they'd taken captive from Wake Island." They were also given an American medical officer, but he had no authority and little medicine to dispense. Kellam says his luck held, and he had little need for a doctor except when some rails shifted and sliced into his hand. He was given medical treatment by a Japanese doctor for that.

There were some kindnesses from the Japanese civilians. Kellam claims they seemed to be "the same kind of animals we were." And he and the others just lived from day to day. "When we weren't working, we were sleeping." One of the Japanese kindnesses came from a man who roasted soybeans and shared them with the POWs while they worked. Another was an occasional bottle of sake to be shared among the men.

When the B-29 raids became frequent, the Jokos and Sokos were put on night detail, and by 1944 even the Japanese children could point to the skies and identify the bombers. Kellam said the bombers headed for Tokyo and Yokohama and passed right over Kawasaki.

In April of 1945 the prisoners were told that their leader, Pres. Franklin Roosevelt, was dead and that the war would soon be over; the Americans would now surrender. After that, the POWs were transferred to Niigata and saw for themselves how many cities east of the mountains had been devastated by American bombing. Niigata, on the west side of Honshu, had its camp in a much better area than the one they'd left. But instead of the prisoners looking healthier, they looked worse than the dead. "They were zombies. The story was that the American commander had bowed to the cruelty and sadism of the Japanese commander. Red Cross packages, when they arrived, were distributed at the whim of the Japanese commander. He was alleged to have beaten one of the prisoners to death just for the delight and sport." At this camp, soybeans were unloaded from barges and pressed into disks. The POWs who ate the disks would pay a price with diarrhea.

But it wasn't long until Kellam and his fellow prisoners were moved back to their old camp, only to find all new personnel. "They were all young, even the guards. We no longer were sent to work each day. We finally learned about the Japanese surrender, but we still hadn't heard about the atom bombs."

A navy plane was the first to spot the camp. The men had signaled from the tops of the barracks. The plane went back to the ship, loaded up with duffel bags containing cigarettes, K rations, shaving equipment, and coffee, and flew back and dropped them. "The commanders even wrote letters to us."

The first American to liberate Kellam's camp was Comdr. Harold Stassen, who was later a Republican presidential candidate. He brought additional supplies to the men, who promptly went into villages and traded them for fresh chickens, eggs, fruit, and vegetables.

When the buses arrived for the men, they departed Niigata for Tokyo and the journey home. After his return Kellam learned that Niigata was one of four cities targeted for the atom bomb, depending on the weather conditions. "The conditions were never right, or it might have been us instead of Nagasaki and Hiroshima."

Ray Kellam spent more than thirty years of his life in the U.S. Army Air Corps (and later the U.S. Air Force) and the reserves. He has recorded his history for his grandchildren, complete with photographs of the areas where he served and the planes in which he flew.

The Eugene Brewster Family

THE EUGENE BREWSTER family lived at Rohwer in one of the two relocation centers in Arkansas for Americans of Japanese descent. The other relocation camp was at Jerome. Eugene and his wife, Edna, worked at Rohwer and took their four children with them. The children, ranging from seven to thirteen, attended school at the center with the children of the Japanese who were interned there. Executive Order 9102, signed by Pres. Franklin D. Roosevelt, established ten such areas for the War Relocation Authority (WRA). These centers were hastily created to take care of transporting and housing an estimated 110,000 Japanese Americans who were, through no choice of their own, relocated and forced to leave property, including pets, businesses, and homes. They carried only bedding, clothing, and a few utensils with them; they were considered by many throughout the United States to be enemies. Trainloads of Japanese from just about every state kept arriving at Rohwer and Jerome throughout the war.

The Brewster sisters, Joyce Stidle and Shirley McFarlin, both of Little Rock, told what they remembered from their childhood in the relocation camp in Rohwer. Joyce is now a Little Rock schoolteacher, and Shirley is a former member of Sen. Dale Bumpers' staff.

"I remember mud everywhere, a lot of it. It was raining that very first day we arrived. There were long buildings covered with tar paper. The barracks were called 'blocks.' There was a walkway—to avoid the mud—made of wooden pallets. The only furniture we had brought from home was a potbellied stove that burned coal. When the coal ran out, we had to burn wood. We stayed in the barracks with the Japanese until they completed our apartments," Joyce said.

For her, the experience was wonderful and part of her happiest childhood memories. "I was introduced to the classics in film while we were there, got to see them all, *Kidnapped, Treasure Island, Hunchback of Notre Dame.* I was in second grade, and there was only one other Caucasian girl in my class, Nancy Millhorn, daughter of one of the other WRA workers. I remember the following year, in third grade, my aunt came to teach there. Her name was Katie Karnes. I just couldn't call her anything but Aunt Kate, so we all called her Aunt Kate, everyone in class."

Joyce said that her brother was the only one of her siblings who ever got into a fight with the other children. She is not sure why it happened, but he got the worst of it from several boys who ganged up on him, and he ended up crying in a ditch. Her parents cleaned him up and told him the next time to make sure he took two or three others into the ditch with him. But it never happened again.

Shirley McFarlin attended seventh and eighth grade that first year (school was year-round) with the internees and hadn't felt she missed out on anything, not even crushes. "You simply developed crushes on the Japanese boys." She didn't reveal any more than that.

"There were no Caucasians my age in camp, not at first. I remember making friends easily, and there were plenty of recreational activities for everyone. In the center of each block was the mess hall, and everyone ate there, and there was only one shower area for each block. We all went together into the recreation areas and sat on the concrete to watch movies projected onto a white sheet. The films were changed often, and we went every time it changed," Shirley said.

"I remember how I felt when I first looked at the tar-papered barracks, the barbed wire, and the flat, desolate country. We were so near the Mississippi River, and the major crop there was cotton. There were no towns close by—the nearest, I think, was about thirteen miles, McGehee—and even when you went into town, there wasn't much to buy."

The camp was large, and Shirley said that she rarely walked its entire length—too much "gumbo," as they called the mud that seemed to be everywhere.

"It was a great adventure." She quickly learned from the Japanese "that I'm no artist and never would be." She laughed, remembering her feeble artistic attempts. But the Japanese were artists. In everything they did, they created beauty.

Edna Robinson Brewster, the girls' mother, now in her mid-eighties, lives with her husband, Gene, four years her senior, at Rogers. She said that before she and Gene worked at the camp, he had taught school and had been a principal. In 1942, after the war began, he didn't need to take a civil service test for the job at Rohwer because he had a master's degree, but she did. She passed, and they packed up their four children and a potbellied stove and moved to the Rohwer camp.

"It was in September of 1942; all Rohwer was back then was a post office and a store. I believe the barracks housed about ten thousand Japanese, but it's been over fifty years, and it's hard to remember," Edna said.

"Gene worked in procurement—supplies—at first, and

I was office manager. Gene made two thousand dollars a year. It's funny that I remember how much he made and not how much I made. I probably made half as much. There were only four Caucasian girls working under me and about sixteen Japanese women who worked there. My assistant was Japanese, and she was wonderful, a real help. I'd never been an office manager before. The Japanese only made twelve to sixteen dollars a month. The work was similar to working for the government welfare office." The Japanese were hard workers, good workers. "They didn't stand around waiting to draw their pay."

At first, the family shared two rooms in the barracks, furnished only with cots. But eventually they moved into apartments built for the workers. The Japanese, however, visited in their apartment many times. Edna and Gene made it a point to make friends with the Japanese and truly liked them and learned from them.

"We all got along fine in the camp, but the rednecks in small towns nearby—and I don't know what else to call them—resented the Japanese. I guess they didn't have much themselves and felt like the Japanese had more than they did."

People had the wrong idea thinking the camps were concentration camps because of the barbed wire and the tower with guards. The truth was that the wire and the guards were to protect the Japanese from those who disliked them. "It wasn't that they were never allowed to go outside. I could check out women anytime I wanted to—when there was enough gas to go into town. But there were some occasions when shots were fired into the barracks; a soldier was hit. It was just ignorance." Her daughters both said they remembered those trips into town and how protective their mother was of these women—keeping people away to protect them.

Mostly, however, it was peaceful, and the Japanese raised their own food and introduced her family to many new and different vegetables.

"There were forty-two blocks and a common laundry and bathroom center in each block. At night, you didn't want to go to the center, so individual families had their own 'pots,'" Edna recalled. The following morning it would be interesting to see everyone out on the boardwalk taking their pots with them to empty them. They'd nod and speak, accepting the reality, adjusting to it.

When the Brewsters moved into their own apartment, they had their own kitchen but could still take their meals at the mess hall if they chose to do so. However, if they ate in the mess hall, they had to turn in their food-rationing coupons. "Since the Japanese didn't have their own kitchens —one Caucasian cook with many Japanese cooks under him cooked for the entire camp—a lot of the women would come and use my kitchen. I learned to love rice. I still cook it more than I do potatoes." One of the Japanese women kept house for the Brewsters while Edna worked. "She cleaned house and ironed for me. I did our laundry." Edna paid her sixteen dollars a month, top pay for the Japanese in the camps.

Few Arkansas doctors would come into the camp, so when Edna's son ripped his lip open on the barbed wire, a Japanese doctor stitched him up. "When the war was over and this doctor went back to his home to begin his practice, they burned him out . . . so hard to believe. We kept in touch for a while." It was some time before the camp got a Caucasian nurse and doctor to staff the hospital; the rest were Japanese.

Gene's job included the additional task of interviewing the Japanese to find out where they wanted to go once the war was over. "I took one trainload of five hundred back to California, and I stopped in Denver, Colorado, to visit my brother on the way back. He was furious. He thought we should have sent them back to Japan. Most of them had been born right here in the United States."

While at the camp, Eugene Brewster taught night classes in geology; before coming to the camp, he had applied for a commission to teach aeronautics. When his commission finally did come through, he was given the option of staying at the camp, and he decided that's what he wanted to do.

"Our kids liked the experience, and because we did this, they'll never be prejudiced against any color or nationality. They learned to judge everyone as individuals."

Joyce and Shirley indicated that this was true, not only because of the camp experience but also because their parents were so liberal in their thinking for the times.

Jim Langford

A T NINETEEN, JIM LANGFORD was an army infantryman
with the Ninety-ninth Infantry Division, the 394th
Regiment, Company I, First Platoon, Third Squad,
taking on every job from rifleman to assistant squad leader.
The infantryman was a foot soldier, sometimes engaged in
hand-to-hand combat with the enemy. "In combat, a
rifleman knows only what is happening in his immediate
area, and what goes on as close as fifty feet away, he probably
won't see or even care. We had no idea the Battle of the
Bulge was going on." Of all the soldiers sent overseas during
World War II, 7 percent were combat infantrymen. However,
of all casualties incurred by soldiers sent overseas, 70 percent were combat infantrymen, a staggering statistic.

Langford went "on line"—into combat on the front line
of the war—for ninety-one days on November 10, 1944. I
Company hiked about seven kilometers to an area northeast of Losheimergraben, Belgium, and relieved a company
of the Sixtieth Infantry, Ninth Division. Langford and his
squad were about a mile inside German lines. The line
was at the International Highway—one of the few roads
through the dense forest—and they camped in foxholes a
mile to the east.

The Ninety-ninth Division was stretched for twenty-two miles. It was two miles to the nearest soldier outside of the company (185 men) before the fight, and the First Platoon's two-man foxholes were stretched out three hundred yards, ten feet apart; one telephone line connected them with the company behind them. This was an area with no roads, just forest trails and fire breaks. "We learned how to do things. There was no hard fighting, just a lot of patrol."

Some men were lost to pneumonia and trench foot, and one soldier was killed on Thanksgiving Day when he stepped on a land mine during patrol. Langford's platoon was soon relieved on the outpost line, and about December 1 the men were moved to an area south of Losheimergraben on the south flank of the Ninety-ninth Division line. The town of Losheim was visible to the front of the platoon, even through the dense forest. This was the famed Losheim Gap through which Germany had invaded France and Belgium three times in history: in 1870, 1914, and again in 1940. Here Langford received word that his daughter, Patricia, had been born on November 23. After a week the men were moved back to Bucholtz Station, where they constructed cabins for quarters. "We thought we were in seventh heaven," Langford noted, "hot food, warm fires, cabins, no patrol, and all the comforts the Ardennes could provide." Though they were considered in reserve for units on the front line, there were no troops in front of the division except Germans.

"On December 15, our good life came to an end," he wrote in his memoirs. The Second Division and a combat team of the Ninety-ninth Division were attacking through the center of the American lines toward the Roer River dams. Langford's group was sent north and east of the twin towns of Krinklet and Rockerath to support this attack.

They camped in foxholes about three miles north of the towns.

In the early morning of December 16, they received a heavy artillery barrage, but were well dug in and didn't suffer many casualties—"half a dozen or so wounded is all." It was part of the German assault that began the Battle of the Bulge.

That afternoon, the men were told to prepare to move to the front; the Third Battalion, 393rd Regiment, had suffered large losses of men and was surrounded, and Langford's group was supposed to relieve the pressure and retake some of the lost positions. "We started over a forest trail before dark, but darkness arrived before we had got very far. It was an eerie feeling walking up that trail because we had no idea what was going on or what we were supposed to do." They reached the battalion headquarters after dark without much trouble. But the foot soldiers could hear the Germans and could not figure out why they had been allowed to go forward without fighting. They found out early the next morning.

On December 17, the company started an attack to retake the positions lost the previous day. "We hadn't gone very far when we bumped into the Twelfth SS Panzer Division, attacking to try to take Elsenborn and trap us. With the number of Germans and the tanks we could see, we knew we were in a bad situation, so we broke off the attack and returned to the 393rd's headquarters." One man was killed and another wounded.

Before noon, a skirmish line was ordered to go up a hill and try again. "An I Company BAR (Browning automatic rifle) man said to me, 'Let's go, too.' So we did. I guess we knew we were surrounded and wanted to take another crack at the Germans before it was too late."

But their move was unsuccessful, and Langford moved back down and learned they were to fight their way out to the west. On the way, the men underwent artillery fire, mortar fire, tank fire, and small-arms fire while passing through a company of the Second Division that had been placed in a blocking position across the trail.

"Capt. Charles McDonald was commander of the company, and he states in his books, *A Time for Trumpets* and *Company Commander,* that about two hundred men passed though his company, the remnants of a battalion plus Company I. We had been one thousand men the morning of the day before. To give you an idea of the intensity of the fight, six Congressional Medals of Honor were awarded to men fighting in the area, and untold numbers of slightly lesser medals for valor were given."

The noise from firing shells was unbelievable. "You can't describe it. It was continuous, not [just] happening for five minutes here, five minutes there. It was constant movement, retreat and attack for three days' fighting behind German lines." They spent the nights of December 17–18 on the reverse slope of a hill, in slit trenches just to get below ground level. The company did no fighting but could see a firefight to its left. The noise alone was bad enough, but with the addition of the terror and exhaustion, Langford's squad had a very rough night.

On December 18, the men were dug in on the crest of a hill above a deep draw running east to west and were in a blocking position against the Germans. But the men had no idea the Germans had mounted a big offensive over a sixty-mile-wide area. "We thought this was just a spoiler attack to try to stop the American attacks on the Roer dams." The unit was again pushed out of position and moved to the north.

They moved along a hedgerow and passed an abandoned halftrack; a U.S. P-47 strafed the Americans. "I got under the halftrack, pack and all, but after the plane had passed, I couldn't get out." Langford laughed at recalling his buddy having to dig him out.

The group met with G Company, 395th Infantry, on a trail north of Krinklet, and were given K rations and directions to Elsenborn Ridge on the northern end of the German advance. They proceeded west, then south around Krinklet and Rockerath, and dug in along a road from Wirtzfield to Elsenborn. "We had arrived on Elsenborn Ridge. This was destined to be the north shoulder of the Bulge battle."

About fifty yards behind American lines was a steep, wooded knoll with a water tower on top and behind it an antitank gun situated to fire down the road toward a bend. "We expected tank attacks most any time as the Twelfth SS Panzer Division was trying to capture Elsenborn and its road network. We were under constant fire from artillery, mortar, screaming-meemie rockets and snipers. One man caught the pin of a grenade that was hanging on his jacket on a barbed-wire fence. The grenade exploded, killing the man. We had several direct hits on foxholes by the artillery fire."

F Company, 393rd Regiment, relieved them here, and I Company moved back toward Elsenborn. The next night, I Company moved to the extreme north flank of the division, rejoining its regiment.

Langford's squad was located on the forward slope of the ridge, just under the crest. Only small bushes dotted the hillside. Langford remembers his foxhole was the fifth from the extreme north end of the 394th Regiment line. "While we were situated on this open hillside, the Germans were across the valley in the woods. We couldn't see them, but any time we moved, it brought down some kind of fire." The Germans, still trying to break through and capture Elsenborn, continued to attack but were not successful, mostly because of American artillery fire. "The battle wasn't won at Bastogne. We stopped them here."

The north shoulder of Elsenborn Ridge, according to Winston Churchill and other World War II historians, was the decisive area of the battle. If the north shoulder had not held, the German army would have captured Liège, Belgium, and possibly Antwerp, thereby cutting off the American First and Ninth Armies and the British Twenty-first, and would have prolonged the war.

It was here that Langford was promoted to assistant squad leader after several men left the line due to combat fatigue and personal problems in January of 1945.

About two hundred yards down the slope toward the woods and the German line was an old underground bunker deemed suitable as an outpost for I Company, and about fifty yards farther down the slope was the German outpost, at the tip of a small clump of trees. "We could hear them, and I suppose they could hear us. We could not see them, but they could see us very well. We could not go too far from the outpost during daylight hours because any movement during daylight alerted them and brought down some kind of fire. We tried several times to capture prisoners from the German outpost, but they could see us coming and left before we got there. We had no hard fighting after New Year's, but constant patrolling and lots of incoming artillery fire and sniper fire. Both sides patrolled heavily, and men were lost on both sides. It was very cold, and snow was waist deep in places. And being constantly in sight of the Germans led to some uncomfortable times during January 1945."

During this time on Elsenborn Ridge, the company received several replacements, including a forty-two-year-old and an eighteen-year-old who didn't even know how to load his rifle. This was not a good place for these replacements to be.

The platoon was on this open ridge throughout January of 1945 in the bitter cold and snow, "the worst winter in the area in many years." About February 1 the platoon moved to help finish "flattening out the bulge." There were casualties from mines and booby traps but no firefights, and the Germans had moved back. Other divisions were attacking across the front, so the platoon returned to the Elsenborn Ridge positions and picked up the dead from a January 15 patrol. They remained in Elsenborn one day and then moved north and east of Losheim to relieve other units. They were again in dense forest in the middle of the Siegfried Line and within shouting distance of the Germans.

Langford's group walked into this area and carried only three days of K rations. They stayed eleven days. Because of steep hills, deep snow, and no roads, the men had trouble getting supplies and did go hungry at times.

I Company was relieved and moved back to Bucholtz Station, ending Langford's part in the Battle of the Bulge. Except for a few hours on December 15, the group had been on the front for ninety-one days.

Langford also saw heavy action as he crossed the Remagan Bridges in March of 1945 and the Danube River in late April. He crossed the Danube under the leadership of Gen. George Patton and got to see the Bavarian Alps.

Langford's medals include the World War II Victory Medal, the Belgium Victory Medal, the American Campaign Ribbon, the Belgium *fourragère* (the Ninety-ninth Division was cited twice by the Belgium government), the Rifleman

Medal, the "ruptured duck" or discharge pin, the Presidential Unit Citation, the German Occupation Ribbon, the Good Conduct Medal, the Bronze Star, the European Campaign Medal with three bronze stars for the three battles fought, and the Combat Infantry Badge, "which raised our pay ten dollars a month."

Norma Dodson

NORMA BONHAM DODSON was sixteen and lived in Lubbock, Texas, when the Japanese bombed Pearl Harbor. She and her younger sister lived with their widowed mother in a small three-room apartment.

After high school, Norma and a friend applied for jobs with Western Union and got them. They had to travel by train to Springfield, Missouri, for their training on the teletype. It was the central training area for the region, and neither of the girls had been away from home and certainly had not ridden a train by herself.

"She's still my lady friend. Her name is Joy Miller now, and I cherish all these years we've had. She lives in Oklahoma City, but we're still close and stay in touch. On that train ride, we soon discovered we were not by ourselves. It looked like a troop train. Of course, back then just about all the trains were troop trains to some extent. Soldiers were always traveling, and they got priority seats. But Joy and I found seats, and I'll have to say, the men were all nice to us. We'd neither one had any experience around men—much less men in uniform—but we were fine."

Norma, now sixty-nine, still shows the beauty she had as a girl, and at almost eighteen, she must have drawn quite a bit of attention from the young men aboard that train. But there is a quality about Norma that exudes a ladylike gentility. She is not aloof, just reserved. It must have been that quality that was recognized even by the youngest of the soldiers. Neither girl exchanged addresses or agreed to write to the men, but they did talk to them, and the trip passed rapidly.

When they arrived in Springfield, they learned they had been given very nice rooms in a private home. "I remember I had never seen a lump of coal, and this house was heated by a coal furnace. I remember being taken into the basement and being amazed by the coal being shoveled into the furnace. In our apartment, we had gas heat, but Charlie's [her husband's] family had a wood stove for cooking, and they may have heated with kerosene; I don't remember."

The girls lived and trained in Missouri for six weeks until they had mastered the teletype. "We both could type, but the teletype was different, and there were so many spaces, so many abbreviations to learn. I don't guess they use those things now. Anyway, my mother didn't even have a phone back then, and I couldn't call her to talk to her or tell her I was homesick. I wrote her penny postcards. Joy and I enjoyed being there, but we were both glad to get back to Lubbock."

When they returned, they were assigned to the four to midnight shift at the telegraph office. Their office wasn't small; it had several machines.

The girls were cautioned about one machine in particular. "It was to be given priority over all machines. It was the one used for the air base just west of town. We were just a few miles from Reese Air Base, and when that machine had a message—and it could come in from anywhere—we were to give it priority. We were to go to it first and see to it that the wires were delivered to the base immediately."

Norma remembers that the messages for the air base were filled with numbers, and that meant she had to be very careful as she typed. "We were extremely conscientious about our care in transcribing numbers. We were so afraid we'd transpose one."

But even more clearly than the base's messages, she remembers the pall that fell over the telegraph office whenever word was received that a serviceman had been wounded or was missing in action. And there were a lot.

"Charles and I were just friends, but I remember when he was wounded in Europe and a message came through. We weren't engaged or anything at the time. I wasn't on the shift that received the message, and I didn't have a phone, so I didn't know until I went into work. On our shift, we had four who delivered the wires, a redheaded girl—she was the best—and three boys. They delivered the messages on bikes, and they had to do it quickly. In fact, I've often thought since then, there was no way they could have delivered the wires and been any help or comfort to the person receiving the telegram. They just delivered them—didn't stick around. Now it seems sort of cold, just delivering a message and leaving that way."

When she learned of Charles's wounds, the war became much more real to her. She later learned that he had been carried to safety by a Mexican from east Texas. His name was Blas Tenorio. "We became good friends. Charles took me to meet him and his wife after the war. They even named their first child after Charles, calling her Charlene. They had started a grocery business. They did real well for themselves. We still keep in touch."

Charles was part of the infantry that kept pushing the Germans back, one of the heroes of the Battle of the Bulge.

"I kept writing him letters, but as a friend. It wasn't a romance, not at first." After Charles received a "Dear John"

43

letter from his girlfriend telling him she was married, Norma's letters of encouragement became more important to him. She sent him packages of cookies and candies along with her letters, and their friendship blossomed into a romance by mail. "I remember for my eighteenth birthday, Charles sent me a Bulova watch. He'd sent the money to mutual friends [of ours] to buy it for me. I was thrilled. I still have that watch. It's all rusted out inside, but I keep it as a memento for sentimental reasons."

"I just kept working at the telegraph office. My younger sister got married before I did. But when Charles came home after the war, we were married that September. I kept my job for a while. I think I worked there for about five or six years altogether."

Norma said a married couple ran the telegraph office, and turnover was practically nonexistent, not like today's jobs. Only one serious mistake occurred during the war that she recalled, and, thankfully, it wasn't hers. "I don't remember exactly what it was, just that it was so important to get those messages delivered on time. The man didn't get fired, so it must have been justified somehow."

She had no social life during the war except for work-related events such as picnics and Christmas parties. "I dated only one guy from the air base, but it didn't amount to anything. My sister and I were pretty sheltered, and we weren't all that interested in the boys stationed there. We thought they were pretty rowdy." And the men she worked with were 4-F, and they treated her and Joy like little sisters, protected them.

She did recall there being a USO, but she didn't volunteer much. She said that the girls who dated the boys from the air base wore nylons, which were gifts from the fellows and very difficult to find during the war because nylon was used for making parachutes. Soldiers had priority when it came to purchasing nylon hose, and they often used the stockings to barter for commodities or services, the same as they did with cigarettes, or they gave them as gifts. "I don't even remember being that clothes or fashion conscious at the time. Most of the girls I remember, if they were really light skinned, just painted their legs with leg paint."

Norma said that her family was continually running out of sugar because her mother was of the old school—big on desserts at every meal. All their sugar coupons were used, particularly when her mother sent packages overseas.

"I remember standing in line for Camels. I didn't smoke, but I had a friend who did, and I used my coupons to get her cigarettes. Really, I don't remember making any sacrifices during the war. I do remember that Charles wrote to me, never complaining in any of his letters. And it was a long time before I realized how rough he had it, but he protected me from all that. When I heard he was in the hospital, I wrote to him immediately. It was months before that letter reached him, but he had written to me in the meantime, so my next letters reached him more quickly. It was a long wait, though, between letters."

After Norma Bonham and Charles Dodson married, they had two daughters, Charolette and Cecilia, and then had eight grandchildren; Norma hasn't had much spare time to look back to World War II.

Jack and Dottie Larsen

JACK AND DOTTIE LARSEN were high-school sweethearts in Kansas City, Kansas, when World War II broke out. Dottie doesn't remember thinking about the war that much at sixteen, at least not until Jack enlisted in the navy.

"We were engaged before he went in, and his mom had to sign papers for him to enlist. After he went in—in June of 1942—I got a job in a doctor's office as a receptionist. I had worked at a cleaners, too."

In June of 1943, before Jack finished his pilot training at Lambert Field, Dottie visited him in St. Louis, and he told her they were going to be married or she was going back home. They got married. "I was worried that he'd be found out on base and get kicked out of flight school. He wasn't supposed to get married until he graduated. I knew if he got kicked out, his mother would never forgive me."

Fortunately, she had packed a white dress for her visit, and she was married in that dress, but she insisted that they be married by a minister, not a justice of the peace. "We had to ride all over St. Louis on the streetcar to find a minister who could marry us on short notice. It was a minister of the Christian Church, and his wife stood up for us. Names were published in the newspaper when you got a license, but no one ever found out about us. I wore his ring around my neck on a chain until he graduated."

The honeymoon consisted of a cruise down the Mississippi on the *Admiral* for dinner and dancing. She said Jack was as nervous as she was about being discovered, and when a superior officer came up to them while they were dancing, they both thought the jig was up. But it was just a military matter. Another sailor had something improperly sewn on his uniform, and the officer asked Jack to draw his attention to it in order to avoid an official reprimand.

"After about three days, I had to go home and face my parents and his and tell them we were married. After he graduated, he went to Pensacola, and I later joined him before he was sent for more training at Great Lakes Naval Base. He was practicing carrier landings on Lake Michigan."

That first year, they went home for Christmas by train, and it was so crowded she had to sit in the conductor's seat, and Jack had to stand out in the cold between two cars of the train. "He got pneumonia but recovered. After that he was sent to San Diego for assignment, and I joined him there. He was assigned to a squadron in Seattle. He had to cross over to Kirkland, Washington, every day by navy launch to get to work."

A typical wartime incident occurred when Dottie reserved a hotel room in Pasco, Washington. They checked in and got to their room only to find three other couples from Jack's squadron occupying it—one couple in bed. With the housing shortage, possession of a room was permitted for only three nights, the couples had no rooms of their own and were simply "squatting" there until the Larsens arrived. The three other couples all immediately went in search of living quarters, and one couple was fortunate enough to move in with a minister's family.

"[The couple living with the minister and his family] really did have the best situation. They had cooking privileges. They were limited to bathing three times a week, but that was because the septic system could be overloaded, with disastrous results. We got a room staying in a sheriff's house, no cooking privileges. There were only three places in town that served food. One was the drugstore—ham-salad sandwiches; the hotel, I'm not kidding, served chicken a la king six nights a week; and there was the Chinese restaurant. We rotated where we ate, and once in a great while, the sheriff's wife would bring us in something. We were there for three months, and finally just before we left, we were permitted to go on base for our evening meals. We'd take a bus, eat dinner, and then go to a movie on base. We didn't have a car, of course, and you went everywhere by bus."

Jack trained in gunnery for three months there. They then moved back to California for his night-flight training.

"The women in the squadron were all close friends, and we helped each other out. When the guys trained on night flying, we all played bridge all night to keep the same hours as the fellows. They'd come back and pick us up, and we'd walk home in the dark, no street lights on at all. But this time Jack and I were living with a schoolteacher, and we did have cooking privileges. The mayor's house was huge, and they gave housing to more than one couple, and that's where we all went to play cards every night."

Dottie was going through her "experimental" cooking stage. And with meat rationed, she had found some hamburger and was going to make a meatloaf to surprise Jack—and surprise him she did. She couldn't find any onions at the store except for some funny-looking small ones which she supposed were California onions. "Remember, I was from Kansas and pretty naive. I prepared the meatloaf. We each took one bite and couldn't finish it. I've never in my life tasted anything so awful. I mentioned it to the lady we were rooming with, and she said I'd probably just used too much garlic. I told her I didn't cook with garlic. She finally convinced me that what she smelled was garlic, and that while cooking with garlic was uncommon in my neighborhood in Kansas City back then, it was quite common in California."

Housing shortages became worse as they moved from pillar to post, from one base to another. They once lived in a converted brooder house where Jack had to squat down to get into the kitchen, and where Dottie had her first experience with goats and goat milk. One time they even shared a Quonset hut with another couple. "I was always the one who had to find us a place to live in a time when there just weren't any places to be found."

By June 1944, Dottie was pregnant with their first daughter, and Jack was ordered to go to the battle front. He shipped out, and Dottie went home to stay with her parents and have the baby. "She was born October 13, 1944, and both sets of our parents were in the delivery room. They sent Jack a wire through the Red Cross, but he never got it. I had sent out birth announcements to all the wives I knew in his squad, and one had sent the birth announcement on to her husband. That's how Jack found out he had a daughter."

Jack was back in California when the baby was six months old, and Dottie went to join him in Modesto, California, and to look for a room for them. She left the baby with her parents. Every place she found refused to rent to them because they had a baby, but one couple finally took pity on her for having to be separated from her baby. Dottie was permitted to heat the baby bottle and baby food, but otherwise had no cooking privileges.

Jack made a career of the navy, staying in over twenty-two years. They added three boys and another girl to their family.

Dottie remembers World War II as a time of change, but not as the worst time in their life together. "The worst time was when Jack was in Korea. He was gone for eighteen months, and I was left behind with a seven-year-old, a four-year-old, a two-year-old, and a baby. That was the hardest time for me."

Jack Larsen is a much-decorated navy pilot. In twenty-two years of service he received the Distinguished Flying Cross, Air Medal, Presidential Unit Citation, National Defense Service Medal, American Campaign Medal, Asiatic-Pacific Medal, World War II Victory Medal, Philippine Liberation Medal, Philippine Presidential Unit Citation, European Service Medal, Navy Occupation, United Nations Service Medal, and the Korean Service Medal.

"I graduated from high school in Kansas City in June of 1941. In 1942, I heard about this navy program you could join if you could pass the tests. My dad had died when I was real young, and my mother had remarried. I'd always used my stepfather's name, but never had it legally changed. I had to be legally adopted before I could go into the navy as Jack Larsen."

He had eight weeks of civilian pilot training at Marysville, Missouri, and then went from there to Athens, Georgia, at the University of Georgia for fourteen weeks of preflight school.

"It wasn't like today—they couldn't get by with it now, but back then, they did everything they could to break the fliers—they wanted only the cream of the crop, and they made it so rough you'd quit. But I made it, and from there I went to Lambert Field to learn to fly navy planes."

He went into the navy as seaman, second class, taking home fifty dollars a month. It was during his pilot training that he decided he couldn't be separated from his high-school sweetheart any longer. They were married secretly before he completed his training.

After he received his wings and his commission as ensign in September of 1943, at the age of nineteen, he went to Daytona Beach and specialized in combat aircraft and dive bombing. He sent for Dottie again, and she had to take the train alone from Kansas City. "I got to the station to meet her—no bride. I looked all over, questioning everyone. Finally this colored man—that's what you called African Americans then—he asked me if I was looking for a white woman. I told him I was, and he pointed me to the colored waiting room of the station. Dottie had gotten off the train, had seen these open doors, and had gone in to sit down and wait. She didn't know what was going on. She was the only white person in sight."

After two months in Florida, Jack was sent to Great Lakes Naval Base and trained in landing a plane on a carrier. He had to qualify with eight safe landings on the USS *Wolverine* on Lake Michigan. "I lost an engine once and had to ditch."

One time, as he took off from a carrier in San Diego, he went through a wave but managed to keep the plane going long enough to get back aboard. And once he lost the tail of his plane before he ever took off. As a navy pilot of so many years, he kept up his log book, neatly dated with tiny printing carefully recording each flight. "I learned to fly the F-4Fs, the navy Wildcats, but they changed planes to the SB-2Cs, and I flew those, too."

The ship he served on was an escort carrier, the *Natoma Bay*. The ship was 498 feet 10 inches long and 65 feet wide and had an average speed of eighteen knots. "We called it the 'Kaiser-Coffin.' Built by Kaiser Shipbuilding in Vancouver, Washington, it was christened on July 20, 1943."

The *Natoma Bay*'s record was impressive, carrying four admirals through five major Pacific combat operations in ten separate actions. The ship received eight battle stars and even survived a hit by a Japanese kamikaze pilot.

Larsen flew sixty combat missions. He shot down a Japanese Zero and sank a Japanese torpedo boat. He flew twice in the area where George Bush, who later became president, flew and was shot down. Bush is said to have been the youngest pilot officer of World War II. "I don't know how old he was, but I know I turned twenty-one in November of 1944."

Larsen flew at the battle of Leyte, at Leyte Gulf, and in the invasion of Mindoro, Luzon, and Iwo Jima.

"I was very fortunate that in every invasion, I was assigned over the landing beaches, mostly strafing and bombing so our troops could land. We never had any one D-day; we had many D-days on a smaller scale. Aboard that ship, we all sweltered and stunk, not like today. The ship had wooden flight decks, and we did everything on our planes manually. We cranked our wheels up and down, lowered our tail hooks, and cocked the guns, all manually. Later we went to the F-6Fs, all hydraulic, but not then."

The ship usually sent out four torpedo bombers and eight fighters at a time, but at Leyte Gulf, there were eight ships, so at least eight times that many planes took off.

"We knocked out cannons; we fired rockets. The first time was at Iwo Jima. For their day, they were pretty accurate. I hadn't been trained in rocket firing and was off the first couple of times. But you learn accuracy pretty quickly."

He never told Dottie of the dangers of takeoff and landing on a small carrier. He told her it was a "piece of cake." For years, Dottie repeated the stories he'd fabricated for her benefit, and he stood by, letting her. She marvels at the fact no one ever called her on them. "I was so naive."

Jim Carpenter

J IM CARPENTER, NOW a retired lieutenant colonel, served with the Fiftieth Signal Battalion, Third Armored Division, during World War II, and received the Bronze Star and other medals. He says the Bronze Star was pinned on by Maj. Gen. J. Lawton "Lightnin' Joe" Collins. Carpenter seems quite unimpressed by his medals; his wife, Teena, has kept them and taken care of them to pass on to their sons. He was impressed, however, by all the skills he acquired while serving his country, skills that prepared him for when he left the service.

"In May of 1944, I was a second lieutenant attached to the Seventh Corps with the Eighty-second Airborne. Lightnin' Joe was our commander. I arrived in Liverpool in March, but I wasn't told anything, and you didn't ask. I didn't know what to expect, but I didn't have long to wait. In May, I was pulled in to replace a battalion officer killed in a practice run for the D-day operation. *I* didn't get any practice at all." Carpenter was among the men who landed at Utah Beach. He said he also had the privilege of serving in other major battles: France, Belgium, Germany, and the Battle of Ardennes. It was this action, his wife said, which earned him the European Theater Ribbon with the five battle stars and the bronze arrowhead.

"We sailed out on the battleship *Nevada,* but storms on June 5 were so bad they canceled the landing and invasion, postponing it until the next day, waiting for the seas to calm." With the heavy seas and the anticipation of battle, no one got any sleep the night before the invasion, particularly those waiting in the landing craft (Landing Ship-Tanks, called LSTs).

"I remember the number 936 on ours and another LST with two diesel engines lost one [of its engines], and since we had a motor officer on board, they passed the engine in to us, and we welded it for them and passed it back."

In the early morning hours of June 6 the *Nevada*'s gunfire could be heard pounding away at the beach, signaling the beginning of the invasion.

"I wasn't the only one who hadn't seen any practice. The naval officer in command hadn't, either. He dropped a cable and [an anchor] to winch himself off, and we made about three passes before we could land the craft, but the tide was coming in, and I finally said, 'We're gonna get off, and we're gonna get off dry.'" They completed their landing successfully with the trucks, trailers, and jeeps "safely on the beach. We were luckier than those at Omaha Beach, and we had fewer losses. German eighty-eights could be heard all around us, but we knew as long as we could hear them, we were OK. One eighty-eight went into a truckload of gasoline cans, and it made a pretty good fire."

A bulldozer was seen clearing the beach of vehicles. The driver had a rough job, a job Carpenter didn't envy. "He was stuck there. We could leave the beach."

His outfit's job was no picnic in the park, either; the men were to lay cable before the roads and mines were even cleared. He recalled the liberation of Sainte-Mère-Eglise well, saying the troops just kept moving, moving. This was the town so often depicted in films with the paratrooper left hanging from the church tower in the square. To this day, he said (just having returned from the fiftieth anniversary of D-day, June 6, 1994), they have a dummy hanging from a parachute, changing it as it weathers—a grim reminder to the townspeople of all the casualties suffered during that invasion. The horror of the bombing during the invasion was beyond comprehension. The small town of Saint-Lô was bombed by twenty-five hundred bombers. "General McNair was killed in that raid by friendly fire, and 97 percent of Saint-Lô was destroyed." It is such remembrances that help him understand the reality of the horrors of war, the countless victims, and how one day, June 6, 1944, could have been the turning point in so many lives.

By the time he reached Germany, troops were out of everything, including food.

"I remember spending Christmas night of '44 in a bombed-out hotel. We found some radio parts and rigged up a couple of radios. So we did get to hear Christmas music. I'll always remember that night and hearing Bing Crosby singing 'White Christmas.' You don't forget those moments."

Jim Carpenter and his wife, Teena, were among the many veterans who took part in the fiftieth anniversary of D-day, traveling aboard the *Queen Elizabeth II* to the town of Saint-Lô. They rubbed shoulders with such celebrities as Walter Cronkite, Edwin Newman, and Bob and Delores Hope. "When Walter Cronkite spoke at one of the ceremonies, he received a standing ovation."

The trip to Saint-Lô did produce one coincidence. Out of eighteen hundred passengers aboard the *Queen Elizabeth II*, about half were WW II veterans. "I ran into the battalion motor officer from aboard our ship. He lives in Atlanta now. What was so strange about the meeting is that fifty years ago, we'd only spent about forty-eight hours together, but we both remembered." During their week's stay, that was the only person the couple ran into that Jim knew from his first Normandy tour.

The Carpenters said they were both visibly moved by the formation of the ships commemorating the anniversary of D-day. "The *Queen Elizabeth II* was joined by hundreds of other craft and individually owned boats, one after the other. They just kept coming. It made you remember the first time when every boat was called into action. I think just about every boat owner came out that day, just like the first time."

Kurt Tweraser

KURT TWERASER WAS born in the small railroad town of Wels, Austria. It was an important railway junction during World War II and the site of an aircraft factory and an airport—three prime targets for American bombers.

His father was a clerk in an appliance store and expressed almost no interest in politics; instead his interest lay in his collection of stamps. He was an avid philatelist. "If I had to label him, I'd say he was a socialist, but neither of my parents were particularly political. They didn't like Hitler, but not from any really solid knowledge in the beginning. It was just instinctive. My mother was not educated but had a very sharp mind. She was a Catholic and had been raised on a farm. I remember the first time she saw a photograph of Hitler. She said, 'Anyone who combs his hair like that—there's something wrong.' So, while her reasoning may not have been sound, she instinctively disliked him and distrusted him."

Tweraser's own dislike of Hitler stemmed from his awareness of the changes in his hometown after the Nazis marched into Austria. "I never liked the marching, the shouting, and the goose-stepping soldiers. I remember my mother was a maid for an officer's family from the old monarchy. She would take me with her sometimes. It was March 13, 1938, I was only about eight, but I remember hearing a lot of noise and going out on the balcony to see what happened. There were lots of people in the streets shouting and happy. But inside that house, I saw the colonel with tears in his eyes. I remember that vividly. I remember wondering what could have happened to make people in the streets so happy and him so sad."

A good student in school, Tweraser was always near the top of his class, if not at the top, but he didn't like being ordered around or being told he must belong to the Hitler Youth as he was expected to do.

"When you were ten you were supposed to join, like the Cub Scouts. When you were ten your parents also had to decide whether you were to go to the main school—four more years to prepare you for an apprenticeship—or into a preparatory school for the university, a program of eight more years. My parents couldn't afford to send me to the preparatory school. I had to go to the main school to become an apprentice."

There was a third alternative, however; the Nazis would take the very brightest in the school and pay for their education at the school the Nazi party chose. "I should have been selected from my school, but I'm glad I wasn't. The teachers were the ones who recommended the students, and they didn't recommend me—I wasn't 'proper' material." He wasn't even permitted to enter the apprenticeship he desired. He'd wanted to be a forester, but the Nazis told him no. Instead, he was placed into bookkeeping.

He was told to join the paramilitary Hitler Youth organization, which was made up of many groups, each with its own specialty, but he decided there wasn't room enough in his life for two dictators. His mother was enough, he said, laughing.

"I skipped school the entire two weeks that we were supposed to receive [Nazi] training. But at the end of the time, I began to worry. If you didn't receive your certificate showing you'd taken training, you didn't get to advance at school, either."

So, Tweraser sought out a friend of the family, a man who led one of the youth groups and who could get him a certificate. The friend agreed to the request but told him he'd have to become a part of the Hitler Youth group he was leading, a fire brigade. The fire brigade was required only to extinguish fires; for its members there were no indoctrination and no military posturing. Tweraser joined the fire brigade to get his certificate and was permitted to stay in school.

In the spring of 1944, the bombing by American planes began. At first, no one took the American bombers seriously. They believed that German air power was stronger and would protect them. Tweraser would stand with other people looking up at the skies during air raids. "I remember watching the American planes being shot out of the skies in one of the earliest raids. They had no fighter plane protection on that raid. But after that, I remember the bombs whistling—people were still standing around and watching. There were many casualties. We'd usually have about a ten-minute warning, but not always."

The air raids were the worst part of the war. By the fall of 1944, schools were closed, and Tweraser was an apprentice bookkeeper at the aircraft factory, a primary target of the bombers. "One time, I recall running out when we heard the warning, and I hitched a ride on the back of a truck. I just clung by my hands, hanging on for about ten minutes to get away from the factory site." He managed to hold on through sheer determination and fear, but another time, he climbed into the tower of the church just up the street from his house. He wasn't thinking of the danger, only of the experience, sort of like watching a movie, not really being a part of what was going on.

But by the fall of 1944, the Germans were growing desperate, and because of their need for manpower, they conscripted young boys and old men, all that were left. Tweraser was inducted into a paramilitary organization and was trained in the use of hand grenades, bazookas, and other weapons.

"It was the *Volkssturm,* and we got three weeks of intensive training. Our transportation was bicycles. We formed, about two hundred of us, a bicycle company of old men and children. Our instructors were SS officers, mostly drunk, and we were being trained to go to the Bavarian border to fight Patton, who was approaching. It was totally irresponsible. We'd go out each day on our bicycles, riding in daylight on the open road when the American bombers controlled the air and could easily bomb us. We'd ride to the Inn River."

One day German officers came to take them to battle. The officers simply shook their heads at the pitiful crew, concluding that they'd need more experienced men than these to go up against Patton's Third Army. "So we were just sent on back home. I continued working in the aircraft factory until we were liberated by the Americans from the Seventy-first Infantry."

During the U.S. occupation of Austria, Tweraser took advantage of the opportunity to make friends with the Americans. "I remember the time in the afternoon when they came in. It was 2:30. I went home—my parents were not there—and I took two bottles of schnapps. I approached the Americans and had my own black-market operation going. I would keep them furnished with liquor, and they'd give me Chesterfields and Lucky Strikes, the most popular form of exchange. After that I could trade cigarettes for anything I wanted."

Tweraser said the Austrians, until they were occupied, knew almost nothing about the Americans and had more or less looked upon them as "big children who lacked discipline. They couldn't get over—in fact were amazed—that they could win the war with so little discipline."

He, like the rest of the townspeople, was very much aware of the concentration camps. "We may not all have known what they did at each of them, particularly those in Germany, but we had a camp not five miles outside town. When the Americans liberated it, we saw the results. We saw these 'corpses' liberated from that place coming into town looking as if they came from another world." The townspeople did try to help them—then. Only those who lived during that time knew the futility of trying to help sooner.

"No one can ever tell me atrocities didn't happen. I know they did. I also had an uncle who was sent to Buchenwald and died there. He was a Nazi, but he drank too much and wasn't careful of what he said. The official cause of death for him in 1943 was reported as pneumonia. Everyone knew that pneumonia was a euphemism in those camps. There were lots of deaths from pneumonia. People knew."

Tweraser, after the war, attended the academy and then went on to the university in Vienna where he met his future wife, Gene, who lived in Washington, D.C., at the time. They fell in love but had to correspond for two years before they could marry and he could emigrate to the United States in 1962.

Edward Hooks

E DWARD HOOKS, NOW seventy-two, lives on the same family farm where he grew up as a child before World War II in a Catholic community about fifteen miles from Stuttgart, Arkansas.

Arkansas farms played an important role during World War II, and the 840-acre farm in Edward Hooks's family flourished—with a little help from German and Italian prisoners from nearby Stuttgart. "I went to Camp Robinson at Little Rock when I was drafted. But when they found out about the farm, they told me I could do the country more good back home. They classified me 2-C and sent me back."

Because he was the only son and the oldest in the family, his parents would have felt a real hardship if he had gone into the armed services. "I had two kid sisters, the closest was five years younger. We grew cattle, hogs, soybeans, rice, wheat, just about everything." For the duration of the war, Hooks continued to report every six months to Camp Robinson, only to be told his war efforts on the farm took priority. He remained on the farm, wearing denim instead of khaki.

Farmers were needed more than ever. C. Calvin Smith, in his book *War and Wartime Changes,* reports a farm population in 1940 of 667,000; the state's farmers dwindled to

292,000 by 1944. By 1943, at least 19,700 families had left their farms, and as a result, 8,170 farms and 428,528 acres of land were idle.

"I was just nineteen. Our farm was just six miles from the air base. They had a compound for prisoners of war there, and they needed someplace to work these fellows, and we had a place where they could work. We had both Italian and German POWs from time to time, and they worked for us for a year or so. I'll have to say that the Germans were the best workers. The ones that worked for us were from Rommel's North African Panzer Divisions—doctors, dentists, lots of professional people, jewelry makers, artists. They came from all walks of life, but they worked hard." The Germans were grateful for the work. The Italian prisoners were a different matter. "They didn't like to work. Production went much slower when they worked. They were paid for their work, receiving $2.50 a day." Some of them spoke English, and it wasn't difficult to communicate. And they were well guarded. "They didn't make any attempt to get away. The guards would sometimes forget they were even guarding them. One time, a guard laid his gun down and walked off to talk to someone. One of the prisoners picked the rifle up and took it to him." Each day a farm truck would pick the POWs up and sign them out, and each night they would be returned.

When the German prisoners took a break, the talk invariably would turn to airplanes. They would sit in a circle and talk about planes, particularly bombers. "They had been shown propaganda films of German planes bombing American cities. They thought they would come over here to a country devastated by bombing. They'd keep asking us about where the cities were that were bombed." Some breaks were spent in singing and playing instruments.

"They had accordions or guitars. Their singing would make you want to cry sometimes. You could tell they were homesick, just like some of our boys must have been. Most of them didn't know any more about what was going on in Europe than we did."

The proximity of his farm to several area camps and bases brought lots of men to the area who were serving in the armed forces. "We had soldiers in our area from all over the United States. We'd bring them home for Sunday dinners. Everyone did. We'd even drive them to a church two miles from the air base until the chapel there was completed. That took about eighteen months."

He said his family "got a kick out of how some of the boys from cities out east like New York and Philadelphia were so ignorant of farming. Some of them thought potatoes grew on bushes. They would actually take soil, put it in little pouches, and send it back to their families. They couldn't believe what they saw."

Once the war ended, the prisoners of war were given passage home. Some of them kept in touch for a while, but eventually, they lost touch altogether. In 1975, though, Edward Hooks and a group of farmers took their wives on a tour through Germany and the Rhine country. "We found out one of the Germans in charge of our tour had been a World War II POW and had worked on a farm owned by one of our group. That was something."

Thad Eatherly

J UNE 6, 1944, known commonly as D-day, began in Normandy at sunrise and ultimately resulted in the capture of thirty thousand Germans by the Allies. On that day the Germans, also, captured many of the invaders. But a large number of servicemen, including many airmen, were captured before D-day. German prison camps, "stalags," were filled with Britons, Americans, and prisoners from many other countries. Those captured prior to June 6 had no knowledge of D-day, but they eventually received word of this Allied victory through contact with underground organizations or with more recently captured prisoners.

Thad Eatherly of Fort Smith was a technical sergeant with the Eighth Air Force in England. He had trained and taught pilots in the United States, but on this mission, he was a turret gunner. His plane was a B-24 Liberator, which was shot down over a coastal area of France, near Lille, not many miles from the English Channel.

Ironically, it was his twenty-fifth and final mission. He was the third-ranking pilot of the plane's nine crew members. The attack tore the four-engine plane's tail section off, killing the tail gunner. The other eight crew members survived the crash, all parachuting to what they believed was safety, a farm field. "I'll never forget that day," Eatherly, who is now a semi-invalid, said. "It was April Fool's Day—April 1, 1943. We came down in that field and ran to a haystack, or what we thought was a haystack. It was filled with German soldiers."

He was a veteran of many "tidal-wave" missions, secret continuous waves of bombing strikes on Libya's oil fields, which were a major source of oil for Germany. But before his final mission, the Germans had cracked the Allied mission codes and were waiting for the American attack. As a result many bombers were shot down.

Eatherly hurt his back on that flight over France, and the injury went untreated while he was held captive. Because of that, he has lived with back pain for more than fifty years.

After capture, he and the crew were taken to a civilian "sweat camp"—labor camp—where they were held without medical care for thirteen days before being loaded into a boxcar with other prisoners and then sent on a "death march" to Germany. "Dandelions were all we had to eat for days. Those who survived went to Stalag 17-B, and it can't be described." He mentioned the movie *Stalag 17* with William Holden. It didn't begin to show all the horrors.

"I was just a twenty-one-year-old cotton picker from Bay, Arkansas, still wet behind the ears."

He weighed 138 pounds on the day of his capture. When liberated, he had wasted to 72 pounds. "But I'm in pretty good shape for all I went through."

He remembers little of the last two weeks of his captivity. He only knows the story as it was told to him. It seems his buddies had saved his life by their quick thinking. Eatherly had been so ill, he looked dead but wasn't. A doctor and Bill Perry, a flight engineer and pilot, both prisoners, conspired to keep him alive by concealing him among

the bodies on the "meat wagon," the truck where dead bodies were amassed until they had a full load for disposal.
"They tended me daily," he said—long enough for the
American rescue of prisoners in May of 1945. His friendship with Perry has continued over the years, and Perry was
a special guest at Eatherly's fiftieth wedding anniversary a
couple of years ago. After the Americans liberated the camp,
Eatherly was sent to a French hospital and then sailed home
on the battleship *Rheims.*

He is a retired steamfitter and currently active with the
Veterans of Foreign Wars, ex-POWs. He and his wife, Ethel,
have two children, Kenneth and Brenda, along with five
grandchildren and great-grandchildren.

Eatherly is a frequent patient at veterans hospitals; his
health problems are directly attributable to his captivity and
lack of medical care during the war. "He was forced to stand
in the snow in his bare feet," his daughter, Brenda, said,
referring to her dad's circulatory problems. But Eatherly had
no complaints. He said he'd do it all again if he could. "You
were proud to serve your country."

Hollis Vice

H OLLIS VICE, NOW a resident of the Wesley community in Madison County, enlisted in the Eighteenth Field Artillery in 1939, shortly before World War II started. At the time, the Eighteenth was a horse-drawn unit, and Vice, fresh off his family's Oklahoma farm and in need of a job, was no stranger to horses or to working with his hands. He began his military training in the army's saddle-making school.

It was a time of great changes in the tactics of war, one of which was switching to greater mechanization. Horses were being dispensed with and Vice was sent for advanced training at mechanics' school, where he learned to work on and drive just about every vehicle the army used.

For Vice the actual beginning of the war was delayed until 1944. He and his unit were being billeted in England while extensive preparations for the continental invasion were made. On D-day he was supposed to land on Utah Beach, but high winds caused the landing craft to drift south during the approach, and he and his unit found themselves on the south end of the designated landing area. There was one advantage—little opposition from German troops who had been expecting nothing so far south. "At this time we were attached to the Second Rangers. After we accumulated enough support we began moving inland through the hedgerows to cut off the Germans." What is now referred to as the Battle of the Hedgerows took place amidst dense hedges that grew atop ten-foot-high dirt banks, each enclosing an area the size of a city block. Part of a centuries-old farming practice to stop erosion and mark property lines, the thick hedges made movement extremely difficult and helped conceal the withdrawing German soldiers. "No doubt, [the hedgerows] were grown to act like a fence, because you could not crawl through them. The army finally had to put blades on the front of the tanks—it was a digging process for a long way. When we started through those, it was one time you knew you were really in the war because you'd be on this hedgerow, and the Germans would be in the next hedgerow over. We fought for miles and miles in this way."

Vice recalled shooting at German soldiers, taking aim at the swastikas painted on their helmets. "I got criticized for this. I was expert enough that most of the time I hit that swastika on the helmet, and they said it made a terrible mess out of the head that was in it, so they asked me to quit aiming there." At the same time, the Germans were taking the Americans' steel field wire and stretching it across roads at neck-height to decapitate soldiers riding at night in jeeps with the windscreens down. American soldiers retaliated by welding hooked metal pipes to the front of vehicles to catch the wire. They then decorated the pipes with German heads or skulls, but General Patton put a stop to the grisly fad.

The Battle of the Bulge started in the winter of 1944 when the German army launched a massive offensive on orders directly from Hitler. The intent was to drive Allied forces back to the coast and into the sea. Vice's unit was on the northern part of the Belgian border with the British army. No longer a conventional artillery unit, they were now equipped with 4.5-inch rocket launchers—his battalion fired more rocket and 105 mm Howitzer ammunition rounds "than any other battalion over there," according to records kept at the time, and took the most prisoners of war.

Like many units during this battle, Vice's got separated from the main Allied force. "From that time we were actually hiding out from the Germans. We went down south, and communications were very poor. We knew that we were behind the lines: the Germans had passed us by already and had gone."

Vice vividly remembered the bitterly cold Christmas Eve of 1944 when he was given a .50-caliber machine gun and a bazooka and was assigned to shoot at tanks at a crossroads in a small Belgian village. The Germans had assembled almost every available tank for the westward drive and Vice just happened to be in their path. After stopping an American jeep and arresting the "GIs" aboard—who were German soldiers dressed in U.S. military uniforms—Vice returned to his post.

"Very shortly after that, here come the tanks. I've got my bazooka ready, waiting until one gets fifteen feet from me so I can shoot right in the middle of the tracks—that's the penetration point. The tank came to twenty feet of where I was, to where the street turned off, and he turned. And in a little bit, here comes another and the same thing happened. All night long they did that—there must have been two hundred of those tanks that night. They turned and went towards Bastogne. That was my Christmas night."

It wasn't the only close call he had. After barely outrunning one German tank, Vice saw a second coming directly at him. He dove into a foxhole and watched in amazement as the tank continued to head for him. "He runs his track over my foxhole. Right over me, on top of my foxhole. And then he kind of paused, and he went on. At that point I was quite scared. Then after he went on, I realized I had survived." Vice was uninjured. On another occasion he saw an 88 mm tank shell narrowly miss hitting his hand. Still later, blinded by the flare from a tracer bullet, Vice found himself in a Paris hospital for two weeks until his vision was restored. He then returned to his unit at the front lines. Although a part of his formal medical record, the injury did not qualify him for a Purple Heart. Vice estimates that he lost a couple of dozen friends in the war—many the result of a direct shell hit to the foxhole they were in. He survived a German gas attack—later claimed to have been an error—and volunteered for dangerous resupplying missions during the Battle of the Bulge, traveling at night, without lights.

And there were other kinds of hazards. Vice nearly froze to death after one extremely cold night in December of 1944; and, despite their K rations, troops also faced starvation as a result of the difficulty of moving supplies through the frozen and snow-covered landscape. Vice recalls shooting two elk when the soldiers had nothing left of their rations except "dog biscuits," hard, dry crackers which were discarded more often than eaten, except in emergencies. "That was the day our commanding officer came to where we were around the fire and said, 'Boys, it looks like we've lost this war.' That's how bad it was. It had looked like it to us for a long time before then."

Still, they kept moving and hiding, scrounging fuel from abandoned vehicles, and fighting. They reached Bastogne two days after the Germans had removed thousands of prisoners of war and one day before forces under the command of General Patton arrived.

A week after the official cease-fire, headquarters sent instructions that soldiers who had served the longest could be sent home, and Vice's high number, plus his luck in a drawing, allowed him to ship out from Cherbourg. "There were some terrible times, but I know that I was not the only one there—I was not the only one that suffered," Vice said of his war experience, remarking that he has "closed the closet door" on a lot of painful memories. Still, he bears no ill feelings toward the Germans.

He told a story to explain:

"We'd gone through Mannheim and got to one place, a crossroads. Here were hundreds of German soldiers marching down the blacktop towards us. Somebody calls for them to surrender. In the confusion over whether a German officer's movement meant he was going to surrender or start firing, the Americans began shooting, and within minutes, hundreds of German soldiers lay dead. I started checking to see who was alive, who could be moved out as prisoners of war. Two or three guys came up from another unit and started getting prisoners, and I turned to look at the Germans I'd turned over to them, and one of the GIs had shot about seven of those young fellers. I got to looking at them, and they weren't no older than me, and they probably didn't know any more of what their involvement in that war was than I did, and probably didn't have anything to gain out of it. Talk about their atrocities, and here my fella was murdering them—and they were already wounded. I never did figure, like any other wars, that any good came out of it. If it did, the good's all passed me by."

John J. "Joe" Leroux

J OHN J. "JOE" LEROUX of El Dorado and Little Rock was a staff sergeant with the Second Platoon, E Troop, Thirty-sixth Squadron of the Eleventh U.S. Cavalry Group. He put in his three years of duty in World War II under orders that were always "subject to change, because 'Hell, soldier, that's just the way it is.'"

Leroux learned early in 1941 about career changes. As a freshman at the University of Arkansas, studying journalism, he was accepted for pilot training in the navy's V-7 program and thought he was headed for a flattop. The recruiter said there was only one more test, an eye test, which would be over in a couple of minutes. It was also over for Leroux's dream of becoming a pilot: he was colorblind.

Leroux went back to his books as the papers he'd filled out were sent to the round file, but he knew his service was coming up soon. After the Japanese attacked Pearl Harbor, he just couldn't stick it out in school. In September of 1942, he closed his books, gathered his papers, slammed out the door, and ran headlong into his professor, W. J. Lemke. As each gathered the papers they'd dropped, Lemke asked where the young man was going. Leroux answered, "I'm going to war, Mr. Lemke." The professor's parting shot was, "Well, don't forget to write, and don't get your butt shot off."

Leroux said he wrote Lemke many letters and didn't get his
butt shot off, either.

He enlisted in the army where his colorblindness presented no problem. He was sent to Camp Barkley in
Abilene, Texas, as a cavalry soldier, but not the Custer kind,
the armored kind. His training in Arizona and California,
where he was plagued by heat and snakes, put him in good
shape to battle in North Africa where his unit was headed to
help Gen. Omar Bradley and Field Marshal Montgomery
of the British Eighth Army put the squeeze on Erwin
Rommel's Afrika Corps. But it didn't happen. The Bradley-
Montgomery team had already completed the job before
Leroux's unit even got there. So they were sent north—
another abrupt change—to the Continent to tangle with
Hitler's panzers and infantry, arriving on the line shortly
before the Battle of the Bulge, which began December 16,
1944. The Battle of the Bulge was the last German gasp, and
it almost succeeded in driving the Allied forces back to
the English Channel, and that would really have changed
history.

Leroux and his armored artillery went in to the line
December 11, 1944, five days before the German attack was
launched. The Eleventh Cavalry Group was assigned to hold
the northern sector of the Bulge. The group and Troop E of
the Thirty-sixth Squadron did hold, and Leroux recalled,
"Somebody asked the CO [commanding officer] how we
would be able to get out of this mess, and he told them, 'feet
first, soldier, feet first.'"

The mission to hold was no drill, and Leroux remembered how Bastogne held out and was rescued by General
Patton's Third Army. The weather cleared and United States
planes and the British Royal Air Force blasted the Nazi
hordes, and the day was saved, but at heartbreaking cost.

In his own words, Leroux recalled the battle, but with

sensitivity, he left out the gory details, although he remembered them well: "Our route took us to Rouen, east to Soissons, north into Belgium, and northeast to the southern border of Holland just north of Aachen, and across the Cologne Plain to Düsseldorf on the Rhine River. North of Düsseldorf, we crossed the Rhine at Wesel and moved on to Coesfeld, Münster, Minden, Hannover, Langenhagen, and into the Klotze Forest near the Elbe River, where our action ended.

"At the end of the fighting, May 8, 1945, I was a platoon sergeant, Second Platoon, E Troop, the Eleventh Artillery for the squadron. [The position of platoon sergeant is one of the least enviable posts in a line outfit since he is out front with the platoon leader, usually a second lieutenant, also an unenviable assignment. Both posts had among the highest casualty rates in front-line fighting, with more deaths as well.]

"In the fighting across Europe, we saw action with the 102nd Ozark Division, the 84th Woodchopper Division, 5th Armored Division, 17th Airborne Division and the 6th British Airborne Divisions, all a part of the Nineteenth Corps, Ninth Army under General Simpson."

At the end of hostilities, Leroux was assigned to the Twenty-eighth Cavalry, a reconnaissance squadron, for occupation duty in Berlin. At Templehof Airdrome, Berlin, he witnessed the first meeting of Gen. Dwight David Eisenhower, Allied Supreme Commander, with Marshal Georgi Zhukov, Russian commander of the First Belorussian Army, which liberated Warsaw, conquered Berlin, and accepted the surrender of Germany along with Allied forces in Reims, France, on May 7, 1945. Leroux recalled that each of these men commanded the largest armies ever assembled in the history of the world.

Leroux, after pondering about the good and the bad of his part in this war, had these comments: "The good was landing in Scotland to be greeted by kilted Scottish bagpipers playing 'The Yanks Are Coming,' attending the Biarritz American University in Southern France where I got nine hours of college credit toward my degree, and then being able to stand at the iron bars of the fence before Buckingham Palace on May 8, 1945, to be greeted by King George VI and Queen Elizabeth and their daughters, Princess Elizabeth and Princess Margaret, as the victory in Europe was announced.

"The bad includes the mud, snow, and cold of the 1944–1945 winter, so cold the fuse heads on our artillery shells froze; the hungry, abandoned children pleading for food along the roads in France and Belgium; crawling through an orchard to repair a blown-out gun line, opening the door of a burned-out German halftrack, and having the skeleton of a German soldier fall on me; and the sad fact that a goodly number of the men who marched with me into Scotland did not march out of Europe with me."

Helen Brandenburger

"THEY ALSO SERVE Who Only Stand and Wait" was not Helen Brandenburger's motto during World War II. She stood all right, on her feet for sometimes twelve and fourteen hours a day, not waiting, but doing what had previously been "men's work."

In 1942 she was teenager Helen Ryder, fresh out of high school. Her eastern accent still strong, she told of going to work at Grumman Aircraft making navy Hellcat fighter planes. "My older sister, Norma, was a plant secretary, and she got me into a training school right after graduation."

She said that the date December 7, 1941, the bombing of Pearl Harbor, was burned in her memory. She was working at the Loft Candy Store in Freeport, Long Island, New York. When the radio announced the attack, she realized that many of her classmates would be joining the armed forces—too young to vote, but old enough to be killed.

"And a lot of them did enlist. I went to work right out of high school for Grumman in Bethpage, New York. I had appendicitis my very first week and ended up in the hospital." She feared she might lose her job, but when she returned, they had a job waiting. They put her on bench work at first, until she was completely recovered.

Workers in Freeport carpooled because of the gas short-age. If she was late arriving on her corner where she caught her ride, they would drive off without her. She had to hitch-hike on several occasions. "But we wore slacks or coveralls with an aircraft badge showing. We never had any trouble getting rides."

Brandenburger remembered that Grumman Aircraft was a male-dominated factory, and the workers were used to having women in clerical positions, not on the line. "At first, the men were always playing jokes on us, the usual thing—being sent to the tool crib for the assembly line and asked to bring a left-handed wrench or left-handed screwdriver." But it was only a short time until the women were accepted as equals.

After her recovery from the appendectomy, she was taken off bench work and soon made her way to the cov-eted position of riveter. "I was assigned to riveting the cowl-ing, which fit behind the propeller of the F-4F fighter plane. This was one of the most needed aircraft since its wings could be folded for storage aboard aircraft carriers." The riv-ets had to be perfectly flush and each riveter was teamed with someone who stood on the back side to make sure riv-ets were flattened evenly with the bucking bar and had no open cracks. Speed, accuracy, and teamwork were essential.

"We stood up for as long as twelve hours a day, six days a week. I'd sing popular songs while I worked." This led to her becoming a part of the Grumman Glee Club, a chorus made up of singers from several area plants. They were the official morale boosters for plants in the area. The singers traveled by truck to appear in special programs during lunch hours to entertain workers. They were paid overtime for entertaining workers on the swing and graveyard shifts.

"But we still had to be at work on time the following day.

We were visited by the big brass sometimes, too. We'd line up on the airfields, and they'd commend us on making our quotas, giving us 'E' pins to wear for excellence."

Some of that brass included pilot Butch O'Hare, for whom the Chicago airport is named, ace pilot Robert Taylor, and many others who came through the training classes and factory to speed up production. "When Secretary of the Navy Frank Knox came through we were all called out to have a rally and to meet him. At these times, we would receive our 'E' pins, and they really meant something to all of us. We did take pride in our work for the war effort."

Usually the routine was unvarying, and the twelve-hour workdays were broken up with two fifteen-minute breaks and a thirty-minute lunch break. Workers learned to sleep during those breaks.

One of the women Helen worked with had a husband who was captured by the Japanese. He made it through the war, and Helen and her co-workers were privileged to meet him. However, he looked like a skeleton after his ordeal and couldn't have been recognized from the photograph his wife carried.

Salaries for the time, particularly for women, were good. Brandenburger even managed to save money. "I had enough to buy a horse and keep it at the stables to ride, and enough saved for a big wedding when I married in 1948."

In addition to working in the plant, she and her friends volunteered at the USO (United Service Organizations) club and hosted dances and receptions for the servicemen. "I wish I'd kept some of the letters from the servicemen I wrote to, probably fifteen or twenty of them." She and the other women were told on August 15, 1945, their services were no longer needed at the factory. "It was a real culture shock trying to find a job out in the real world again. I worked at a lot of jobs including Lockheed Aircraft and the overseas division," she said. Twenty years after the war, after moving to California, her knowledge of machinery—drill presses, sanders, grinders—landed her a good job in Santa Ana.

Mementos from her aircraft factory days are small heart-shaped pendants the workers fashioned from scrap Plexiglas. "That's about all I have left. I used to have a model of the plane I made, but in so many moves, it got lost along the way. We would take home scrap Plexiglas [used in making plane windshields] from the plant and make hearts out of them. We were told not to, but we all did."

Remembering those days is like looking back on a different lifetime, Brandenburger said. It was a safe time on the home front. "It was an exciting time meeting people from all walks of life. You could walk the streets, hitch a ride to work. Maybe it's a shame to say it, but I recall those days as a wonderful time."

Robert and Marilee Curtis

D URING WORLD WAR II, patrol torpedo boats (PT boats) were "ambush vessels, hunters and marauders," according to PT Boaters Incorporated. Assignments also included escort duty, spy transport, commando ferry, leading beachhead invasions, and laying smoke screens. The job of Robert L. Curtis of Springdale was to support the crews of these boats in the Pacific campaign from aboard a PT boat tender, the USS *Varuna*.

"They were small, but fast in—and out quick," Curtis said. "We saw some pretty big times."

Curtis served as torpedoman, first class. On the *Varuna*, he was in charge of the torpedo shop and, with his crew of about twenty-five men, repaired and maintained torpedoes for the PT boats. Depending on where in the Pacific the tender was, the *Varuna* served one to four squadrons of PT boats with eight boats in each squadron.

The seventy- and seventy-seven-foot craft ran on Packard engines for quick power. "We stayed pretty busy. With the facilities on the tender, we could just about build a PT boat." PT boats were made of wood, and the crew of the *Varuna* would saw new pieces of wood to fit the holes made when a boat was damaged by enemy fire. The tenders were also equipped with a cradle to lift a PT boat out of the water for repairs.

"I got lucky today," Curtis wrote his intended, Marilee Hammett. Now his wife, she remembered the V-mail, but said she didn't hear the details of how he "got lucky" until Curtis returned to the United States after the war. While overhauling a torpedo in the shop, a firing mechanism somehow went off in his hands. He was not hurt in the incident.

"We got in a lot of hot areas. We were doggone lucky. It was a real good ship." Two PT boat tenders were lost during the war, but the *Varuna* never lost a man. "We were lucky, very, very lucky. Tokyo Rose [a propaganda radio broadcaster for the Japanese] reported us as sunk twice. We were fired at; we just wasn't hit. Our biggest concern was the kamikaze [pilots who would fly directly into targets] and other aircraft."

The Japanese hated PT boats because the elusive vessels tended to do a lot of damage before being seen. Curtis and the other torpedomen on the *Varuna* were also trained as gunners. "On a quiet day, they would spend at least four hours on a gun, besides working on torpedoes or the boats." The *Varuna* kept a crew on half her guns twenty-four hours a day. And because the ship was often anchored close to shore, each gun crew carried small arms to fight off boarders. The small arms and .30-caliber machine guns mounted on the rails of the ship also took care of any action too close to the ship for larger guns. "Fortunately, we never had to use them for this purpose," Curtis said.

Curtis remembers many nights spent in the gunner position staring at the Japanese but not being allowed to shoot because any gunfire would give away their position.

"Most of the suicide missions took place at night. I guess

the islands looked like ships. The Japanese kept crashing planes into these islands."

For the most part, however, PT boats and their tenders stayed on the outskirts of big battles. The biggest gun on the PT boat was three inches.

Standard armament for PT boats included a 40 mm Bofors cannon, twin .50-caliber machine guns on each side, a 20 mm Oerlikon and a 37 mm automatic, depth charges, four torpedoes, smoke-screen generator flask, small arms, and hand grenades. "The early boats had hardly any arms, but more were added as the war progressed." He saw the original blueprints and arms specifications for the PT boats. "But what was normal, you never saw. No two were alike. They used whatever they could get ahold of." John F. Kennedy, who served off the *Varuna* and whom Curtis knew by sight, added marine anti-tank artillery to his boat. "Then everybody wanted it. They liked to shoot tanks, trucks, and storage buildings on shore."

Some of the PT sailors also scavenged a Japanese suicide boat from Corregidor. "But they didn't get to keep it. It was sent to some big shots in Washington."

"The tender didn't see as much action, compared to the boats," Curtis recalled. "During an attack, we would hide upstream, well camouflaged among the scrub trees on the little islands." PT boats and their tenders stayed close to shore, never making more than a two- or three-day run. The smaller boats stayed near the tenders, depending on them daily for fuel and food.

Curtis left for the Pacific in February 1943 and was involved in campaigns at New Caledonia; Guadalcanal, Rendova, New Georgia, Bougainville, Green Island, and Treasury Island in the Solomons; New Guinea; Luzon and

Leyte in the Philippines; and more. The *Varuna*'s campaigns included the consolidation of the Northern Solomons, February 13–29, 1944; the Bismarck Archipelago operation, March–August 1944; the Eastern New Guinea operation, September 9–27, 1944; Western Carolinas operation, Alau-Kossol Passage, October–December 1944; Luzon operation, Bataan-Corregidor landings, Subic Bay, February–May 1945; and the invasion of Balikpapan, Borneo, July 1–August 29, 1945.

The *Varuna* and its squadron of PT boats were among the first ships at Borneo, and Curtis remembers the landing. "We were there several days before the landing. The water was rough, and they couldn't get the PT boats close enough." The forces spilled crude oil to create an oil slick and settle the waters. Then the mine sweepers cleared the area, and the boats went upriver. "It was a fairly quiet invasion compared to others. They were the last holdouts, and we were expecting the worst. The landing was easy."

Two days after landing, Curtis was able to talk to Australian soldiers who had been on the front lines of the invasion. They, too, had been warned and were expecting shells. "They said that when they let down the ramps of landing barges, they were dreading it, but no one was shot at. 'Thirty minutes later we had a teapot on, making tea,' they said."

The excitement at Borneo started after the invasion. "I heard a commotion but no general alarm. I looked up, and the sky was all lit up like an invasion. On shore, fireworks were going off. The Australians and New Zealanders were going crazy. They shot off everything they could get, and they even managed to set a freighter on fire."

Now seventy, Curtis was only a seventeen-year-old in

Mineral Wells, Texas, when he volunteered. He finished high school by correspondence while in the navy.

"I wasn't ever scared during the fighting; I was always too busy—it was only after it was over and we got to looking around to see what happened."

Curtis completed boot camp in San Diego and was assigned to the torpedo shop at the destroyer base there. He then attended advanced torpedo school and was assigned to the navy yard at Charleston, South Carolina, where he put the torpedo shop into commission.

It was in Charleston that he met Marilee. "I was born in Dallas, she was raised in Oklahoma. And we had to go clear across the country to meet."

After the surrender, Curtis turned down a promotion to chief in favor of returning to the United States. As chief, he would have had to stay with the ship for its return to three more months of duty. As it happened, the *Varuna* nearly beat Curtis home while he waited for military transportation.

In 1950, Curtis enlisted again and served in the Korean war as torpedoman on the USS *Dixie,* a destroyer tender. The *Dixie* also served as the flagship of the United Nations escort and blockade force.

Curtis received military honors including five battle stars, the American Theater Medal, the Asiatic Theater Medal, the Philippines Medal, the World War II Medal, the Occupation Medal, the Japanese Occupation Medal, the National Defense Medal, the United Nations Medal, and the Korean Medal.

Today he is an active member of the PT Boaters Incorporated based in Memphis. The organization consists of eight thousand men who were assigned to PT boats and their tenders during the war and is dedicated to preserving the history of the PT boats.

During World War II, Marilee Curtis was a teenager, not a soldier, but nevertheless, she spent time in a war zone. "Most didn't realize it," she said, "but the American coastline was declared a war zone. More ships were sunk off the East Coast than in battles. We were scared in South Carolina."

She remembers an instance when a German submarine was sunk by American forces just off the coast near Charleston. Among the debris were bread wrappers and newspapers from the city. "The Germans had been in town shopping." The German sailors, many of whom had lived in America before the war, could easily mingle with the townsfolk.

"Ships from France, Norway, Sweden, Great Britain, and all over came in for repairs." She remembered going downtown—only on special occasions because gas was rationed—and seeing sailors from other nations in their different uniforms and hearing their different languages.

While she was on the East Coast, her husband-to-be, Robert, was on the West Coast before being shipped overseas. "On the West Coast, every vacant lot had a gun [search] light, and tall buildings had antiaircraft guns," her husband added. And fake houses, barns, cattle, and trees were put on top of nets to make the area look like farmland.

At the time, Marilee's father was a mail carrier in Hodenville, Oklahoma. As the war continued, the government sent a letter to federal employees asking them to take a leave of absence and take a defense job. The government promised them their old jobs back if they complied, with no loss of time. "Well, my dad was raised in a tin shop and almost had a degree in engineering." He got a job repairing ships, and the family with four children moved to Charleston in 1942.

No housing was available when the family arrived. The

city of ten thousand before the war grew to one hundred thousand. "We stayed in a motel and slept on the floor. They were building houses as fast as they could. We waited six weeks."

Charleston is located on a peninsula between the Ashley and Cooper Rivers. "Ours were the last houses next to the river," Marilee continued. "We weren't sure subs weren't coming up the river." She also remembers unmanned blimps being placed off the coast to interfere with enemy aircraft.

"There were no street lights and the upper half of car headlights was painted black," she said, leaving a strip of about two inches long and one inch high. "Then there was a block warden on every block to make sure homes turned out their lights during air-raid drills. Air raids were expected but never came." Armed guards and dogs patrolled the beaches at night, and civilians were not allowed there.

"There was not enough food in grocery stores," she recalled. Though the family had rations stamps to buy meat and could see cuts displayed in the store counter, store owners said there was no meat. "They said they had to take care of the customers that would be there after the war. We ate what others wouldn't, a lot of potatoes, rice, grits, beans."

Getting fuel oil for heating was another problem. Each household was given a fifty-five-gallon drum of oil which was to see them through the winter. "It lasted about a month." In one period when family members fell ill, the family quickly used the oil. She remembers her mother going before the rationing board, requesting more oil and being turned down. "But somehow we survived."

Robert Curtis fared better on the *Varuna:* "If food

was available, we had it. But it was not always available. Sometimes supplies couldn't get through." At one time, he thought they'd eaten all the goats and sheep in that part of the world. The men on the *Varuna* also ate quite a bit of fish. Several liked to fish, especially for sharks. "PT boats were called the beggars because they were always begging off other ships. Food for the eleven to eighteen men stationed on each PT boat was prepared on the tender and then loaded onto each craft.

"The merchant marines who carried supplies to the forces overseas were heroes of World War II," he said. "Lots of ships were burned and shot. Early in the war, that was their target, the tankers, before they started convoys."

"From Charleston, we could see ships burning in chunks," Marilee added. "The German subs had the coastline covered."

Marilee was only fifteen when she met her sailor, Robert. He was eighteen. They met at Thanksgiving and were engaged at Christmas. "My mother fainted when we told her we were engaged," she said. Robert left for the war in February, and they didn't see each other for two and a half years. Marilee received letters that weren't complete. The mail from soldiers was censored, and some letters would include words or sentences blacked out. In fact, some of the Curtises' photographs from the war still bear the stamp of approval from the censor. Robert remembered one instance when he got past the censors. Marilee didn't know where he was; he was on the island of New Georgia. Robert wrote to Marilee that he was "glad to hear your sister had a new baby, and I thought Georgia was a good name."

"I didn't have any sister close to the age to be having babies," Marilee said, "and my mother and I figured it out."

Upon Robert's return to the West Coast from the Philippines, Marilee received a telegram with three words on it: "Prepare to wed." Forty-nine plus years later, the couple have two children and are grandparents. He is a retired contractor electrician.

Right, *Ray Kellam*

Bennett Brogdon

*S.Sgt. John J. "Joe" Leroux, after digging
artillery pits east of the Rhine River*

Gene Long, Weston-super-Mare, England

Muriel Lawrence, at head of table, *relaxing after training at USO conference, 1944*

Helen Brandenburger, far right (the girl behind her has both hands on Helen's shoulders), *Grumman Aircraft Corporation, Bethpage, Long Island*

Jack Larsen

Otis Eubanks with daughter Mary Ellen and wife, Lois, in Oregon, 1942. A filing shed can be seen behind the car.
Photo courtesy of *Shiloh Museum of Ozark History.*

Sgt. George S. Brewer and Capt. Ernie Deane in Paris, 1944

*Lloyd O. Warren,
photographer's
mate, first class,
at Aircraft
Engine Overhaul
Base (AEOB),
Noumea, New
Caledonia,
September 1944*

Kay Hall, flanked by her father, far right, *and her Uncle Goran,
while modeling her father's hat and saluting her mother*

Standing, left to right: *Elizabeth Hooks (Mrs. John M.), a POW,*
Lorraine Hooks, a U.S. soldier guard, and Mary J. Hooks.
A POW threshing crew is in the wagon and another
POW is posed lying on the ground.

Left to right: *A POW, a U.S. soldier, and an Italian interpreter*
(also a POW) on John M. Hooks farm near Stuttgart

Left to right: *Father Boutcholupi, John M. Hooks,*
and Edward D. Hooks

Rufus Johnson

Lois M. Eubanks

ITLER'S RISE TO power in Germany, Mussolini's control over Italy, the Communist party under Lenin's leadership, and Japan's invasion of Manchuria, September 18, 1931, meant little to folks living in the backwoods of Madison County, Arkansas, in the 1930s.

Twenty miles southwest of the county seat, Huntsville, was the little town of Japton, with Ball Creek just up the road. Narrow dirt roads, traveled by the rural mail carrier and peddlers, ran past family-owned general stores and a canning factory here and there. Family transportation was a stout wagon and a strong team of horses or mules. A rock schoolhouse served as a church as well in Japton. Ball Creek's school and church was a wood-framed building.

Otis Carl Eubanks grew up in Japton. Lois Maude Cunningham lived in Ball Creek. In 1938, the young couple —she was fifteen and he was eighteen—married and moved into their new home.

Otis's father, "Doc" Eubanks, helped cut large trees on the farm, skidded the logs to a sawmill, brought back lumber in a wagon pulled by a strong team, and built the two-room house for them on the Eubanks' family farm. Doc had been born in 1878 and drove a team and wagon until the last few years of his life. "Henry Ford invented the automobile after I was too old to learn to drive," he was fond of saying to his grandchildren and great-grandchildren.

Otis and Lois made a living by helping the family raise row crops and by selling eggs from a handful of laying hens. They carried water from a spring and, when "nature called," they went to an outdoor privy or the nearest bushes.

When their first daughter, Mary Ellen, was born, October 23, 1939, Lois and Otis were aware that German troops had invaded Poland, but it was all happening far away. War was a subject they knew very little about. Lois had completed only the seventh grade, as her family moved from place to place scratching out a living where they could. Otis had gone through the third grade and decided he'd had enough education. After all, he could read and write, so he figured that was enough. Education was rarely emphasized in those days and in that rural area.

Lois's father, Jay Cunningham, subscribed to a weekly paper, *The Kansas City Star,* which came through the mail. Being an avid reader, Jay kept up with what was happening and was a source of information for the whole family. The only radio in the neighborhood belonged to Harve and Maud Ball, Lois's uncle and aunt. Families gathered at the Ball home to listen, especially when the president spoke. It was an event, and even small children knew to be very quiet so grownups could hear through the static on the battery-powered radio.

When Mary Ellen was eighteen months old, Otis and Lois left Arkansas with a group of relatives headed for Oregon in the spring of 1941 to work in the timber industry. "Otis had a cousin in Sweet Home, Oregon, who came back for a visit. He talked about the money to be made and the climate being good. We were excited."

When the party arrived in Vernonia, Oregon, the men found work right away, with living quarters in a labor camp. One dirt street was named Arkansas Row. Lois and Otis lived in the filing shed, where the saws were sharpened. It had a glass roof to give the filers light to work by. For the first time in his life, Otis was making good money—$7.80 a day. He bucked trees before they were cut down. (Notching trees to make them fall where the loggers wanted them to fall was called "bucking.") "I remember washing my brother Commodore's overalls and trying to get the tree resin out of the material. It was like tar. I worked very hard to do it well, but many times I was defeated."

World news was readily available in Oregon, and talk in the evenings centered on European unrest as well as what was happening with the logging operation.

Their stay in Oregon lasted less than a year. Eskell Eubanks, Otis's cousin, learned that his mother had pneumonia and was critically ill. Eskell and his wife, Annie, began to pack their belongings to return to Arkansas. Eskell talked to Otis about his fear of not being able to find his way cross-country. He felt that he and his wife could not make the trip alone. A group meeting was called, and most of them decided to return to Arkansas with Eskell and Annie. Otis felt he should come home because Eskell's mother was his father's sister-in-law; here again, this was a family matter.

Lois cried bitterly. "I didn't want to leave Oregon. For the first time in my life, I was healthy. In my heart I knew that once we left Oregon, chances were that we would never return. I was right. The climate was perfect for me. I was eighteen years old and beginning to see how good our lives might be if only we could stay and work."

Huge forests and waterfalls brought the beauty of nature to her eyes as she had never seen it. Returning to the rocky farmland and scratching out a meager living raising row crops so vulnerable to nature's whims was not to her liking at all. But being a dutiful wife, she dried her eyes and packed their belongings for the trip.

"We owned a 1929 Chevy, so we loaded up and the caravan headed toward Arkansas." On the trip to Oregon and again on the trip home, the group did not eat in restaurants or cafes, nor stay in any motels. Food was prepared beside the road, and the men took turns driving so they would not have to stop overnight. The lead car had the brightest headlights; the others followed its taillights. They took several days to make the journey, arriving home December 5, 1941. By the time they arrived back in Arkansas, Eskell's mother had improved and went on to live several decades longer.

On the long trip, Lois and Otis made plans to move into Fayetteville, where his chances of getting a good job were better. There was little work to be had in the backwoods of Madison County.

On Monday, December 8, Lois and her sister, Vera McChristian, drove to Fayetteville, Arkansas, to shop. Fayetteville was the nearest town of any size, so when people spoke of going to town they meant Fayetteville, not Huntsville.

Lois was driving the '29 Chevy without benefit of a driver's license or, for that matter, much experience. Coming up a hill which crested at an intersection near the Washington County Courthouse, she failed to shift gears and the engine died. "Here is where I learned to put one foot on the clutch and brake while using the other one to hold down the gas pedal." She laughed about this years later, saying she was glad, for once in her life, that she wore a size-ten shoe.

When they stepped inside a store, people all around were talking about Pearl Harbor being bombed. Radios were on in some of the stores. Newspaper headlines told the horrible story. Lois and Vera were so upset, they dropped all ideas of shopping and immediately left for Ball Creek to tell the family the dreadful news. Traveling from Ball Creek to Fayetteville, round trip, was an all-day affair. The roads were rough, washed out, and many times muddy. Even on a good day, thirty miles per hour was top speed. It was almost dark when the sisters arrived back home with the news. The family immediately went to Harve and Maud Ball's house to hear what was being broadcast. They listened as President Roosevelt made his famous "date which will live in infamy" speech.

Otis took a job at Litterell Canning Company in Fayetteville to support the family. He and Lois moved into a rent house one block from the Washington County Courthouse. By this time, Mary Ellen was almost three years old, so Lois got a job at Oberman Manufacturing Company, a garment factory that produced men's pants and shirts. A neighbor took care of Mary Ellen during the day. "I was a machine operator making forty cents an hour. It was a decent wage."

Oberman Manufacturing quickly obtained a government contract to make khaki uniform shirts and pants. This gave jobs to hundreds of women who had never worked outside their homes before and provided incomes for families to rely on while husbands and fathers went into the armed services. It was a great boost to the economy of northwest Arkansas.

Otis received his notice from Selective Service to report for a physical examination along with his cousin and brother-in-law, Calvin McChristian; another brother-in-law, Wayne Harriman; and many other members of the family. The men went in a group to Fort Smith, Arkansas.

Wayne Harriman joined the navy, Calvin McChristian went into the army, and Otis was turned down.

"When a child of about ten or twelve, Otis had been in an accident where he had fallen off a logging wagon, breaking his right arm near the elbow, and the arm had not been properly set or put into a cast. His arm had grown stiff, and he could not raise it above his shoulder. The examiners felt he would not be able to shoot well enough.

"Otis showed the doctors how he could hold a gun, but to no avail. He returned home deeply depressed because he wanted to do his part. He was young and strong and felt cheated out of his right to be a patriotic American by going to war."

As with others who were disqualified, Otis began to look for something he could do for the war effort. He found it quite by chance. One weekend Otis and Lois took the train to Fort Smith and then a bus to the tuberculosis sanitarium on Wildcat Mountain between Fort Smith and Booneville, Arkansas, to visit a relative being treated there.

While aboard the train, Otis struck up a conversation with the brakeman, who told him the railroad desperately needed personnel to fill positions left empty due to the draft. He told Otis where to apply and encouraged him to follow up on his suggestion. "Otis did not waste any time. Early on Monday morning he went for an interview and was hired immediately for the Fort Smith to Monett, Missouri, run. The job required Otis to live in the near vicinity of Monett, Missouri, so we moved again."

A second daughter, Sharon Kay, was born May 12, 1945, while Otis and Lois lived in Monett on Sycamore Street in an old house that had belonged to an elderly lady who had passed away. Her family removed her clothing and personal items and rented the house fully furnished. Later her children sold the house and its contents. Lois and Otis bought a striking clock that hung on the wall for $2.75. No one was sure of the age of the clock but knew their mother had owned it from the time she was married. Today that clock still keeps accurate time, strikes, and hangs in the home of Mary Ellen Eubanks Johnson and her husband, Leroy.

After the sale, Otis and Lois moved to Pierce City, Missouri, into an old two-story brick house. "The house sat in the forks of two sets of railroad tracks. Busy freight trains passed by sounding warning whistles all night and day. It was hard to get the baby to sleep and stay asleep." This was still close enough to the roundhouse in Monett for Otis to keep his job with the Frisco Railroad as a brakeman, but when the house was sold, the family moved back to Monett.

Brakemen rotated schedules which were posted at the roundhouse. However, if extra crews were needed, local theater managers would flash notices on the screen. Many times Otis and Lois would take the two girls to a movie on Saturday night only to see the words *Otis Eubanks report to the roundhouse immediately* on the screen. "We would leave the theater, naturally, rushing home so Otis could get into his starched and ironed overalls, along with his white railroad cap, and leave for the roundhouse. I never learned to starch and iron that aggravating railroad cap." Lois still remembers trying to get the pleats ironed in just right.

While Otis was working for the Frisco, he was required to purchase an accurate pocket watch. Brakemen had to respond on the second, not the minute. In July of 1943, he bought a Hamilton watch which he wore tucked into the bib of his railroad overalls, suspended from a gold chain. The watch cost sixty-five dollars, paid out at six dollars a month. Lois still has the watch, and it still keeps accurate time when wound.

Late one afternoon, Otis was running across the tracks near the station in Monett when his shoe got caught between the railroad ties. He struggled to pull his foot free as the sounds of an approaching freight train got louder and louder. Quickly, Otis bent over and untied the shoe, pulled his foot free, and ran far enough away to be safe. After the train passed, he went back to look for his shoe and could not find it. Knowing he wouldn't be able to buy another pair, he went home, got Lois and the two children, and returned to the site, and they searched until after dark. "We finally found his shoe quite a distance away from where he had left it. It took me a while to clean, wax, and polish it . . . so he could wear it to work the next day."

V-J Day came with great celebration, but Otis and Lois knew it would be the end of a way of life for them. Otis's job would be returned to the soldier who had been brakeman before being drafted. However, it took a few weeks for the Frisco to settle down and actually post the work schedules. Otis's name was not on the list, and he knew it was time to move back home to Madison County.

Rationing was taking place all over the country. An office was set up in Huntsville where tokens could be bought to exchange for goods the family needed. "We had plenty of money to buy what we needed, but the items were so scarce it was almost impossible to get the things we wanted."

About this time an apple growers' association in Washington State set up an office in Madison County to hire workers who would travel across the country for better jobs. They knew poor folks from rural Arkansas made good workers. Otis and several other men in the family went to Huntsville to check it out. They returned very excited about the pay and the opportunities they would have in Washington. Plans were made for eleven of them to travel in

Harold Harriman's one-and-a-half-ton truck to Brewster, Washington. Harold was married to Otis's sister, Dessie, and they had six children. Their whole family was going. Otis planned to go with them, see how things were in Washington, and send for Lois and the two girls. "This seemed like a logical plan, but I was in the early stages of having our third child and was not being very logical. I cried all day while washing, ironing, and packing Otis's clothes. I wanted to go, too. I didn't want to stay behind with our two little girls," Lois recalled.

The women and men all pitched in, killed a hog, skinned it, and cooked the meat. They canned the meat and poured hot grease into the jars of meat to seal them. The truck was packed to the limit and ready to roll at daylight. "Late in the afternoon, Otis came back to the house and said he just couldn't go without me and the girls. I worked all night getting our things ready for the trip. I was so excited that I could not have slept anyway."

The group did not eat in a restaurant or cafe along the way. Stopping to stay overnight in a motel was not even a consideration. "I'm not really too sure we even saw a motel along the way."

A bed was made across the back of the truck next to the cab. "Eight people lay side by side to sleep. Boards had been put on the sides of the truck, and a roof was made out of a tarp with another tarp hanging down the back to close the 'living quarters' inside. It was sort of a makeshift camper." One night Lois woke up and noticed the kerosene heater was glowing red-hot; she shouted to Dan Rawlett, who was sleeping near the stove, but Dan did not hear her. In desperation, Lois kicked him in the head to wake him up. Seeing the danger, Dan grabbed the stove and set it outside. No doubt that saved the lives of all of them.

"Crossing the Columbia River on a huge barge was exciting to Mary Ellen, Sharon Kay, and me. Dessie wouldn't let her kids look out the one window because she thought it might scare them. I put my girls up to the window, and we didn't miss a thing." Some years later, a bridge was built to span the river.

At one point along the way, the truck had mechanical problems, and the group spent all day in the parking lot of a gasoline station. A friendly little red-haired boy visited with them. He was home from school that day. Later everyone knew why he had been home from school—he had mumps. Every person who was not immune got the mumps, men, women, and children, so they arrived a pretty sick lot.

"In Washington we all lived in a labor camp. The men worked in the orchards, and the women looked after the children and stood in lines at the food markets trying to buy rationed items. In the evenings, the men would gather and play music. Otis played a mandolin."

In the labor camp were several rows of buildings where Mexicans lived. Lois had never seen a Mexican before. She was familiar with Oklahoma Indians, but Mexicans somehow seemed foreign to her. "The language was different. I couldn't understand them. At night guns would be shot over there and [there was] a lot of loud yelling and screaming. They also played music some nights and seemed to have a good time. We were scared of them. I kept Mary Ellen and Sharon Kay in sight at all times."

Otis, homesick for Arkansas, decided to build a car for him and Lois to go back home in before the new baby was born. A running gear and frame with four wheels came from a junkyard, the remnants of a Ford Model A. Otis ordered the motor from Sears and Roebuck. Seats were made from apple crates. A used radiator was all Otis could buy. It leaked, but a bag of water was hung over it as they traveled across the desert so they could keep it cool and filled.

"Sharon Kay had trench mouth and could not swallow and had a stone bruise on her foot so she couldn't walk when we loaded up for the long journey. We put all our worldly possessions into our 'new' car and set out once again."

Lois was an experienced driver by this time, so she took over the wheel much of the time even though she was in her eighth month of pregnancy. "I look back now and wonder what would have happened if I had gone into labor on the trip. The doctor advised me to fly, but I just couldn't do it with a sick baby and a six-year-old and leave Otis to get himself home alone." Larry Dale Eubanks was born October 31, 1946, three weeks after Otis and Lois arrived back in Ball Creek, Arkansas. Returning to the family fold in Madison County was comforting, especially because food had not been scarce there during or after the war. The family managed to raise what they needed.

Shortly afterward, Otis, Lois, and the three children moved into Fayetteville, where Otis took a job as a plumber's helper at the University of Arkansas. Lois returned to Oberman Manufacturing Company and was quickly promoted to "floor lady," a supervisory position. "We bought a house, on the installment plan, and fell into the same postwar patterns thousands of other young families in postwar Arkansas followed."

In 1958, Otis died of lung cancer at the age of thirty-eight. Lois remained single, raising the two younger children. She left Oberman, took a course in cosmetology, and opened a beauty shop in her home on Poplar Street in Fayetteville.

Otis's sister, Vassie, went to California to care for the children of a cousin who had a secretarial position in a defense plant.

Lois's sister Lenora had quit her job at Oberman's during the war to go with a friend to California, where they worked in an aircraft factory. Lenora was a typical "Rosie the Riveter" because she riveted de-icing equipment into the nose of the planes. "Lenora made enough money working at the Douglas plant to buy a house for herself and Wayne when he got out of the navy. The house and five acres near Fayetteville in the Mount Comfort area cost $3,500."

Reflecting on her life, Lois said the war had brought many good changes in their lives, even though many loved ones had been lost in battles overseas.

Rufus Johnson

RUFUS JOHNSON, NOW retired at Hogeye, said Arkansas and Oklahoma may have been behind the times in giving fair treatment, wages, and recognition to blacks, but the United States Army was equally guilty.

Johnson was born in the eastern United States and was living and working in Washington, D.C., when he was commissioned into the army. He, in fact, was the first of the domestic staff from the White House to enter the service in World War II. He was also a promising young black attorney —but he said the emphasis there is on the word black.

Distinguished today by being listed in the first edition of *Who's Who in American Law* and twenty other similar journals, he said his abilities have not always been recognized nor rewarded.

Johnson attended Howard University in Washington, D.C. He was the school's first intercollegiate wrestling champ, a pole-vault champion, and a qualified swim instructor and lifeguard, in addition to being the football captain. He worked as a janitor, a pin setter in a bowling alley, a member of a railroad maintenance crew, and as a steel mill worker in Bethlehem, Pennsylvania, in order to stay in college. He graduated in 1934.

"It was during the Great Depression, and there weren't any decent jobs to be had. Ralph Bunche talked me into getting my master's degree in political science. He said if I got my master's he'd see I got an appointment at a college. As it worked out, I received a scholarship to law school and the political science degree was to my benefit."

He passed his bar exam while working as Franklin Delano Roosevelt's butler. He was an officer with the Officers' Reserve Corps, and once the war started, he was called to active duty with the black regiment, the 372nd.

"There were two black regiments established. The 372nd was reactivated from World War I, made up of National Guard units. Then there was the 366th Infantry staffed completely by black ROTC [Reserve Officers' Training Corp] graduate officers." Two additional divisions of blacks, the Ninety-second and Ninety-third, had white officers.

"The 93rd was sent to Japan, and I went with the 92nd to Europe, where we were a major functional unit against the Germans in Italy. I was sent from the 372nd to complete its quota of officers." Johnson was one of ten black officers sent from the 372nd to the 92nd. Of those ten, he was one of only two who survived the war.

He had been prepared well to be sent overseas as an officer. He had received training at Washington and Lee University. However, when the trustees learned that two black officers were at the university, they threatened to withdraw endowments. It was the only time he used his connection to Roosevelt. President Roosevelt told the school, "I don't have time to be bothered with this. They're officers, so train them!"

Johnson had been in ROTC at Howard and had gone into the army commissioned as a first lieutenant. He had a background in swimming and lifesaving, having served as

FDR's lifeguard as well as his butler, so it fell to him to teach every man in the Ninety-second to swim well enough to meet requirements for overseas, since they would be aboard ships that could possibly be sunk. "I was the only officer in the army during World War II to do this. I had to teach them to sustain themselves in the water, at least long enough to be picked up."

But officer or not, it was plain to Johnson from the time of his induction that the army discriminated against blacks, particularly noncoms. "The southern doctors wouldn't even examine the blacks. One man got accepted with one eye, one with parts of two fingers missing. I can't tell you how many went in that should have been 4-F. The doctors simply wouldn't touch them. And if you examine the medical records, you'll find that the doctors, invariably, put the medical terminology for flat feet on the record. It didn't matter if you had flat feet or not; if you were black, you can bet the records show you have flat feet." He laughed as he ended the story.

The Germans in Italy had prepared well for his convoy's coming. They had loaded the Mediterranean with mines, "and we had already lost three or four ships to German submarines on the way. So our convoy stayed near North Africa until the Mediterranean had been swept for mines."

Even aboard ship the discrimination didn't stop. From North Africa, Johnson was sent with his unit to a British ship. "We were sent out from North Africa sort of piecemeal. They segregated the black officers, eight of us, aboard this British ship. Two were chaplains. The white officers ate in the main dining room, but we ate [in a room]off the kitchen. I was pretty mad, and I kicked over our table and asked to see the captain of the ship." The captain, it seems, had made a study—had wanted to follow

American procedures to avoid a protocol problem. He immediately remedied the situation, and the black officers were seated with the whites.

In battle it was no different, according to Johnson. Blacks were consistently ordered into combat where losses were likely to be heavy. It was his division which drove the Germans to the Po Valley, where they finally surrendered. "But not to us, we were black. They surrendered to the Brazilians. They were in the armored division. They had absolutely nothing to do with the surrender or in driving them off the hill. They were more or less a service unit, but they got credit for our work."

He told of several other instances of discrimination: "I was then transferred to command the guardhouse—the black guardhouse—right on the front lines. Never mind that the Geneva Convention said the guardhouse was to be at a safe distance from front lines. We were there, at the only guardhouse to be so close. This was by order of the general. Shells whistled by our heads, and we had to hit the foxholes just like in combat but without ammunition." He then asked for combat. "They knew to do that, they'd have to give me command of a company, and they didn't want to. They put me in charge of black bathhouses for when men came back from battle to be deloused and bathed."

Johnson frequently wrote in his small leather notebook. The tiny record, with painstakingly small writing, contained such accounts as how the British, with shells bursting around them, really did stop for tea every afternoon, no matter what.

Johnson next volunteered to clear mines. "There were no mine detectors. This was done with a trench knife. You went out in the broad daylight and crawled on your belly. I cleared a pathway, and I got a medal for it."

But even in combat, discrimination loomed its ugly head with every turn—over a simple little thing like the Combat Infantry Badge, given to anyone who crossed the line of demarcation into combat. Blacks were denied them unless they had distinguished themselves in battle, and white men decided whether or not they had distinguished themselves. Johnson continued to volunteer for the worst or most dangerous missions. Another way the white officers discriminated was with rotation. After two days of straight attack, your unit was supposed to be rotated. Units under Johnson's command never were rotated.

At one point his company had taken its objective, but the units to his right and left had been pushed back. That meant the Germans could surround him easily. He always stayed in front with his men instead of to the rear. He had just gotten 150 of his own men back to safety when the Germans captured him. Since it was noncoms who captured him, they had no authority to question him, so they walked him back to their headquarters, one behind him with a bayonet and one in front.

"But they hadn't planned on me knowing the territory so well. I had studied every inch on maps. I knew just where the creek was running, and I timed my escape perfectly. Just as I got to the creek bed, I wheeled around and bayoneted the man in front with the bayonet held by the man behind me. My wrestling came in handy to overpower the other one with a choke hold. I did escape, killing them both, and I got back to my own lines."

Eventually, he was wounded by shrapnel, but it didn't keep him down. He had the wound dressed and led the assault by his unit for the third straight day of attack.

In another situation, while holding the North Apennine Line, with no troop movement during the hard winter, just random shooting throughout the day, a Catholic priest had been given clearance by headquarters to pass back and forth, claiming to have parishioners on both sides of the line. One of Johnson's men, illiterate, but far from unintelligent, told Johnson, "Cap'n, I don't like that priest. Every time he comes, something bad happens. One time my friend was killed; before that there was some shelling. I think there's something fishy."

Johnson started to watch more closely and checked after each crossing. His man was right. After each instance, an accurate shelling would occur, consistently resulting in casualties. The next time he left to go back, Johnson approached him, and the priest asked if something was wrong. "I'm taking you into custody, and I'm going to search you," Johnson told him. The priest drew an Italian Beretta from beneath his robe; Johnson shot him three times—to the heart.

Headquarters verified he was not a priest at all, but a spy. He had an accurate drawing on him of every installation and of the locations of food and ammunition to be shelled. "It turned out that little guy who couldn't read or write had been smarter than any of us, including those at headquarters."

Johnson was mustered out at the rank of captain and began his law practice in Washington, D.C. But after two years, he moved to California and studied for the bar there. He passed the bar exam, but soon after was called back to duty, this time in Korea. When his commanding officer learned he was a lawyer, Johnson was appointed Staff Judge Advocate for Fort MacArthur, California, making him the first black man to hold that position.

After Korea, Johnson gained respect as an appellate lawyer. He also achieved renown with the "Peyote Case," winning the suit for the Navajo Indians and protecting their right to use peyote in religious ceremonies. He has long been an advocate of civil rights for all people. Johnson is currently living in Hogeye with his wife, Vaunda, a transplanted Texan.

Donald Lively

NEWTON COUNTY IN northwestern Arkansas is known for its natural beauty and tranquillity but still to this day does not offer much in the way of employment. World War II had a major impact on the county and its population because of the employment opportunities that drew residents away to cities. The war changed Newton County, intensifying the trend for people, especially the young, to leave the Ozark Mountains to make a living. It caused an exodus, giving many families a chance to earn much more money than was possible at home. They traveled to states such as California where there were good jobs in the defense industry. Some of the residents who left during the World War II era were pulled back to the state later by strong ties. While some families were re-established in later generations, others put down roots in their adopted homes. Donald Lively was a teenager who went with his parents to Oakland, California, in 1944. His father went west first, and Lively and his mother followed later by bus. The family returned to Newton County the following year.

Lively now lives in Bass in the southeast part of the county within a few miles of where he grew up.

"The county has changed a lot since those days. There's

not as many people here now as there were then. And most lived off the farm. Most grew cattle and some hogs, and most had a few chickens. The war boom gave residents a chance to improve their financial situations. They could make a lot more money than they'd ever heard of."

Lively was about twelve years old when the war started. He remembered several young men along Cave Creek going off to war. The ones he knew were drafted: "Uncle Sam sent them an invitation."

He also remembers hearing adults express the feeling that most of the young men who went overseas would not come back. However, the Newton County boys he knew were fairly lucky; only a few were wounded and a few were taken as prisoners of war.

Residents received much of the news about the war from radio, although Lively remembers that his family heard about the bombing of Pearl Harbor when they attended Sunday morning church services at Happy Home, which also served as the community school and gathering place. Not everyone had radios, so neighbors kept each other informed.

Most of the young men Lively knew who served in the war were between the ages of eighteen and twenty-three and hadn't started families yet. When the first ones returned, the community held get-togethers for them, such as a dinner at a local church.

One of the stories Lively told was of a man he knew who had been captured during fighting. The former POW used to carry an eight-pound lard bucket full of food with him when he went out for a day's work. Someone asked the man why he wasn't afraid he would ruin his stomach by eating so much. The man replied that he came so close to starving to death while he was a prisoner that he promised himself if he ever got the chance, he would eat as much as he could, whenever he could get it. He and another Newton County POW had survived in part because an Indian captured with them told them which insects to eat.

On the home front, people in Newton County didn't suffer much from shortages and rationing of food and other items because of their self-sufficiency and simple life. Rationing of tires and gasoline affected residents very little because few had vehicles. There were some tractors around. "Our food we grew, so we had plenty of that," Lively said. Sugar was in short supply, but many people, like the Livelys, were in the habit of making molasses for use as a sweetener.

Lively was in California when the Japanese surrendered, and he remembers the scene very well. His family was living in a house rented from some other Newton County residents, whose son, several years younger than Lively, had a newspaper route. After he finished his route, the boy was on the corner hawking papers, and cars were lined up in the streets blowing their horns in celebration.

A monument in Jasper on the downtown square memorializes veterans from the county.

Lloyd O. Warren

L LOYD O. WARREN of Fayetteville was a navy photographer during World War II and served in the Pacific theater. While American forces fought through Normandy in the wake of D-day in 1944, Warren was in the South Pacific aboard a naval ship named for Pres. James Polk. His ultimate destination would be Guam, one of several islands in the Mariana chain east of the Philippines targeted for invasion by American forces.

Warren enlisted in the navy in February of 1942, but before reporting for active duty, he married Ruby Pearl Burks on February 10. He went to San Diego in March, but she stayed and finished school, joining him upon her graduation in May of that year.

Ruby got a job in California at Consolidated Aircraft Corporation and helped build B-24s. She remained there even after Warren went to sea. Once he left, they were not reunited until May of 1946, in Fayetteville.

During World War II, Warren was trained as a navy photographer at Pensacola, Florida, and spent most of the war shooting film throughout the South Pacific. His base of operations was New Caledonia, an island almost a thousand miles east of Australia in the southernmost Pacific. At one point, the navy loaned him to the First Provisional Brigade of the Marine Corps for their operation in the Marianas, three thousand miles to the north.

"We heard about Normandy over the PA system. They said the European joint invasion had been a success." Warren couldn't recall the reactions of the men around him when they heard the news because he was too intent on the mission of retaking Guam. The lightly defended island had fallen to the Japanese on December 10, 1941, three days after the surprise raid on Pearl Harbor.

In June 1944 an American armada had targeted three islands in the Marianas for invasion: Saipan, Tinian, and Guam. To retake Guam meant destroying a Japanese observation tower on a hillside, a tower protected by big guns that made landing difficult.

"Our ship was on the Agat Beach side of the island, and the observation tower was just above Agat Beach," Warren said, pointing to a photo he'd taken from aboard ship of what looked to be an off-center peak of the hill. It was, in fact, a Japanese observation post firmly implanted in the hillside.

Eighty percent of his group eventually became sick with dengue fever while there. The illness, carried by mosquitoes, was called "break-bone fever" because of the pain involved. The only medication they had available to them was the military cure-all—APC tablets, glorified aspirin. "While on the island, we'd just keep going; but once we got to a hospital, we did get treatment."

For American forces, Guam was another hideous blood bath. It took five days of hard fighting before marines and army troops could term the situation under control. In

History of the Second World War, by Time-Life books, the battle for Guam is recounted:

> Yet once again, the Japanese refused to acknowledge the inevitable. Crouched in their foxholes, the Americans in one sector could hear hysterical shrieking and laughter and the breaking of bottles. Then the Japanese came, the officers waving flags, the men brandishing pitchforks, empty bottles and baseball bats. Artillery fire descended on the charging Japanese, and an American lieutenant later described the carnage: "Arms and legs flew like snowflakes. Japs ran amok. They screamed in terror until they died."
>
> The survivors fled back into the swamp whence they had come—to be wiped out by readjusted artillery fire. Even then, the fighting went on for two weeks. And, after Guam had been declared secure (in August 1944), small bands of Japanese held out in the hills, guerrilla style, for months—in some cases for years.

After the action with the marines on Guam, Warren recalled how difficult it was to get back to his home port: "The funniest thing about the loan was, on our return, the Marine Corps just said 'good-bye' and left me on Guadalcanal to get back to New Caledonia the best way I could. I had to wait, but finally hitched a ride on a C-47 naval transport, and then went on to New Caledonia on a marine aircraft."

Upon completing his tour of duty in the Pacific, Warren was sent to Washington, D.C., in May of 1945. In charge of the sorting and processing of photos taken by the military, he had access to film shot by military personnel and made copies of some historic shots of such notables as Pres. Harry Truman, British prime minister Winston Churchill, and Russian dictator Josef Stalin.

Warren is a professor emeritus of entomology and former director of the Arkansas Agricultural Experiment Station at the University of Arkansas. He has a great collection of photos from World War II. He's interested in history and genealogy, and he pursues these interests locally, belonging to several museums and historical societies.

Bennett Brogdon

J ULY 1940 WAS no different than most summers in Arkansas, hot and dry, Bennett Brogdon recalled, but with one difference: he was thinking about enlisting in the armed services before his country declared war and while he still had the chance to pick the branch of service he wanted, the Army Air Corps. "I'd always wanted to fly from the time I was a little, little kid."

Brogdon had graduated from high school in January and already had one semester of college at the University of Arkansas, Fayetteville, under his belt. He was only eighteen at the time of his enlistment and basic training at Randolph Field in Texas. He had a lot of training, basic and otherwise, on three sites: Eagle Pass, Texas; Oklahoma City, Oklahoma; and Garden City, Kansas, all neighboring states. After basic he became a Link trainer on a mock airplane, named after the man who developed it. "That's when you teach instrument flying, train young cadets."

By September 1942, his dream of becoming a fighter pilot began to come true, and he was admitted to aviation cadet training. He graduated in June 1943, receiving his commission as the lowest in the army. "The two lowest ranks are corporal and second lieutenant. And the pay? It was twenty-one dollars a month."

After receiving his "wings," Brogdon was assigned a brand-new C-47 at Fort Wayne, Indiana. He piloted it on its maiden flight to Augusta, Georgia, then on to West Palm Beach, Florida, and overseas via Puerto Rico, British Guiana, Brazil, Ascension Island, Iberia, and Casablanca in North Africa. After this, he headed for his tour of duty in southern England.

The C-47, which he refers to as the "best built plane of the war," was "a very stable plane, no bad characteristics. It would float if you landed in the English Channel. Some crews that went down, reportedly, never even got their feet wet. And you could shoot a pretty big hole in it, and it would still fly."

In England, he flew a C-47 day after day, practicing missions for the D-day invasion. Then, on the early morning of June 6, while it was still dark, he took off with a cargo of paratroopers, members of the 508th Regimental Headquarters of the Eighty-second Airborne Division. The paratroopers jumped over Sainte-Mère-Eglise. "My plane didn't get hit, never did. After carrying the paratroopers, we towed in glider planes—single- and double-glider tows carrying phosphorous grenades. A tow line was hit once, but not the plane."

There were eighteen hundred planes in his "train" with the Ninth Air Force on D-day, but his outfit didn't lose men the way the Eighth Bomber Command did that fateful day. In fact, most of the pilots who flew in his group survived. "The Eighth must have lost forty thousand men."

After D-day, Brogdon flew supply missions. "We were grateful that our hero, Gen. George Patton, had captured three or four drop zones. He saved us a lot of trouble." On some return trips, his unit carried wounded men and prisoners back to England, flying as low as eight or nine hundred feet. Most crews preferred wearing flak suits for protection against artillery rather than wearing parachutes.

After the Normandy invasion, Brogdon flew missions in Holland and, no longer lowest in rank, received his first lieutenant's bars. He received the Presidential Unit Citation for his participation in Normandy and the Air Medal with the oak-leaf cluster for his role in the Holland and Normandy invasions.

Although he avoided being wounded during the war, he did develop acute appendicitis. Peritonitis set in, often fatal in the days before antibiotics. He was shipped home on the *Queen Elizabeth*, which operated at the time as a hospital ship.

Of his hospital stay in New Orleans he recalled, "You didn't get a private room in the army hospital, but I had one. I was dying. But they used me as a guinea pig, tried out a new drug on me—penicillin. They shot me every three or four hours. They'd keep draining the poison, and I lost fifty pounds." After five months in the hospital, he recovered and eventually returned to duty.

With five years of service behind him, Brogdon received his discharge at Fort Bragg, North Carolina, and immediately returned home to enroll at the University of Arkansas on the GI Bill. "After taking four and a half years to graduate from high school, I got through college in two and a half years." He later married Martha Belle Johnson, a true southern belle.

Though retired, Brogdon, now a widower, still serves his community as a member of the Washington County Quorum Court. "And I still fly, but I spend more time on the golf links than in the skies."

John and Jane Rankin

WORLD WAR II was easily recalled by John Rankin: "I served in all three, the American, European, and Pacific theaters. I enlisted in the navy." He was only twenty-three when he "joined up" to see the world. That was in September 1942. He began as an apprentice seaman, then became an ensign, and by war's end was a lieutenant, junior grade. "You might say my career was varied, starting out as an aviation machinist and going on into the gunnery—a communications officer in the armed guard for the army transport ships."

His wife, Jane, recalled, "War was declared after we'd just been married a year. In fact, it was declared on our first anniversary, December 8, 1941."

At the time, John was working in a service station and store for B. F. Goodrich in Clarksville. The young couple was having a rough time financially, so when John enlisted, Jane filled in at his job at the service station. "It didn't last long. They couldn't get tires, couldn't get gasoline, and they finally had to close. So when John was sent for his machinist training in Memphis, actually outside Memphis, in Millington, I joined him there."

The war presented both good opportunities and long separations to the young couple. They met while at the

University of Arkansas; John had graduated from the law school there and had passed his bar exam. He just couldn't make a living at law in those lean times in Arkansas before the war. "That's why he was working at Goodrich, to keep us from starving," Jane recalled.

In the telling of their story, both frequently laughed when mentioning the rough financial times. It was as if they had always known they would have it rough but would survive and prosper.

When Jane joined her husband in Memphis, she found a room in a boardinghouse near Overland Park, a nice section of town. John, who couldn't live in town with her, came in whenever he could, but within six months he'd shipped out overseas—a familiar story during wartime. She was alone and in a strange place where she knew no one but her landlord.

"But the woman I rented from was a wonderful widow woman and became a good friend. She had only one other boarder, a woman she'd known all her life. She also had two sons living with her, but one enlisted. The other was too young. We [the three women] became friends. There wasn't much time for a social life, anyway. After I took the streetcar to work every morning and came home every evening on the streetcar, all I wanted to do was eat supper and read a little while and drop into bed."

Jane was only twenty years old at the time, and the other two women were probably at least twenty years older than she was, but they got along well.

She first worked at Sears and then was fortunate to get a job with Rockwood Insulation for about $125 a month, good money for the times.

It was during his assignment to Greenland, John said, that a "southern boy found out just how cold it can really get. We built landing strips for planes to be ferried across

Hudson Bay, across the ice cap. This was six feet of ice, and the temperature would drop to sixty below zero. But I had loved hunting as a boy, and I got to do some of that. We also set up radio stations, prefab buildings. We were expected to be frozen in for three years, but I guess none of us wanted that, so we got through in record time. We also supplied tankers and broke them out of the ice. We did weather observation, too."

Jane did see John again between assignments, and by war's end she was pregnant with their first daughter.

John had been hauling gasoline to the Christmas Islands and the southernmost Pacific—from the coldest cold to the hottest hot.

"I believe he was in the states when she was born, but he couldn't be there. I had gone home to my parents in Fayetteville to have the baby. I was in the very same hospital room that my mother had when I was born. I thought that was quite a coincidence."

John said that his last ship was an army troop transport with about three thousand soldiers aboard. "We went from Marseille to Manila and learned the war had ended."

Jane said that her memories of the war years have blurred somewhat, but the years following were "plenty interesting, with more ups and downs than a yo-yo."

Roy Bowman

ROY BOWMAN CALLS the Pacific theater of World War II "the unknown war," saying, "I think there was always more interest in the European theater." His memory of what he calls "the bloodiest battle of the Pacific," Tarawa, is firsthand. He is one of the marines who landed safely with the Second Division to rout the Japanese. He recalls in detail the landing on the beach in the second-wave assault of the battle. "It was the twentieth day of November, 1943. I may be an old gyrene, but I remember that clearly."

The Pacific's Tarawa Island, an atoll, was the site of much World War II action, along with the Gilbert and Marshall Islands. The island, not even two miles square, was held firmly by Japanese forces and was the target of an assault by three marine battalions. The landing was made even more difficult because of dodging tide conditions (an irregular tide occurring at certain times of the year) and the surrounding barrier reef. There were six companies of about fifteen hundred men in the initial assault, three thousand in three assaults that first day. According to Bowman, a thousand men died, and many more were wounded.

Bowman was under the command of Maj. Gen. Holland Smith, referred to by his men as "Howlin' Mad" Smith.

Bowman waded onto shore under heavy gunfire and felt immediately his first moments of terror. "I was carrying my M-1 across my chest. I guess it's what saved my life. It was shot right out of my hands and knocked me back into and under the water. I was plenty scared. Then, when I came up out of the water sputtering, right in front of a sergeant, I scared him to death, too."

Bowman laughed, recalling the shock and horror on the face of the sergeant. He claimed that scare was a good thing and that he was grateful for an early brush with death. It acted as a reality check, to prepare him for all that was to follow. With his gun demolished, he was forced to search for another, and he took a carbine from a dead marine.

Marines that day crept along on their bellies, moving inches at a time. "And we were all a little in shock, with those killed and wounded all around us. We were scattered all over, and so we just joined up with four or five men wherever we could. You assumed leadership if you had to; you did what needed to be done with the men you had. It's amazing how men rose to the occasion." Amtrac vehicles saved a lot of lives. These tractorlike vehicles shuttled troops and offered them armored protection.

"In a firefight, you see only about ten feet on each side of you, and you don't know a darned thing about what lies a hundred feet away. But we didn't quit until that island was secured. We kept at it night and day until it was finally over. We took seventeen Koreans prisoner. We had killed all the rest." And the "rest," according to *Seventy-Six Hours: The Invasion of Tarawa,* by Eric Hammel and John E. Lane, was over four thousand Japanese troops.

Bowman said he often thinks of the men who far exceeded any heroism that could have been expected of them or that could have been explained. Courage was just there, all around them. "The men did astounding things. I think the medics assigned by the navy were the absolute greatest. They went right into the water when we landed. They had to dress wounds while they held the men out of the water to keep them from drowning. I remember one in particular. We called him Frenchy. That's the only name I knew him by. He stayed there in that water . . ." As Bowman spoke of this, his voice broke with emotion still intense after fifty years.

He told an amusing tale about one of his seven-man team, a man who was pinned down behind a log, surrounded on three sides. The Japanese kept chickens on the island, and this chicken kept coming up to the trapped marine, drawing unwanted attention to his position. He finally shot it. It made a good story for his buddies, who repeated it every chance they got—the mean fighting machine, the great big marine who destroyed his enemy, a chicken.

An interesting sidelight of the invasion was told in *Seventy-Six Hours,* an account of how Americans determined the number of Japanese to be routed, how many occupied the island: "Because the Japanese had a history of fastidious bathing and hygiene habits, instead of building the usual latrine trenches, they had built wooden latrines on small piers up out over the water—a way in which to use nature's tides to sweep away the waste. Clever, but it permitted strategists to determine the number of forces to be overtaken." American intelligence estimated the number of troops at 4,840. After the battle, the actual number proved to be 4,836.

Bowman's stint in the Pacific included serving in the Marshall Islands and on Saipan. Although he escaped being wounded, he didn't escape illness. "On Saipan, I ran out of cigarettes. I was offered a chaw of tobacco, and I gave in and took it even though I'd never chewed it. It was sweet and burned my mouth, but it was nicotine. Well, I must have stupidly swallowed some of it, and I've never been so sick in my entire life. And to this day, I can't stand to be around the stuff."

Roy Bowman was a sergeant at the time of his discharge, and he returned to Oklahoma after serving from December 1941 to December 1945. He became a radio announcer at KGFF in Shawnee, Oklahoma, before going on to become owner of his own advertising agency in Springdale. He is currently retired and lives in Springdale with his wife of fifty years, Maxine.

William Dunklin

"PINE BLUFF WAS changing before the United States got into the war," William Dunklin recalled. Economic change, in particular, began when a munitions plant was constructed and when the air school opened and the National Guard came into Pine Bluff. People came "in droves" to find work and rental houses—settling most often for rooms.

The main problem, as Dunklin remembered it, was that "there weren't any houses ready. Almost everyone rented out rooms in their homes or even their garages. I know my mother did. She rented our garage, converted to a bedroom, kitchenette, and bath, to a young married couple. He had just graduated from West Point. This was pretty typical because there just wasn't enough housing."

Dunklin told about "Spoonerville" housing that was quickly constructed—small but sturdily built houses for the influx—and how his "sleepy little cotton town" became a military crossroad, "a watershed" surrounded by military personnel. With more military construction and more camps and bases, more people came for jobs and housing. "Those 'temporary' houses are still standing."

When war was declared, Dunklin was only nineteen, a

college student and a member of the Reserve Officers' Training Corps (ROTC). "I was ROTC all four years, and we all talked about the war and whether or not we should get into it. Almost no one wanted to get into it at first, but after Pearl Harbor there was a real turnaround in our attitudes. I was on the college debating team, and we had hot debates on the subject. In fact, when Pearl Harbor was attacked, I was off debating. After that, I'd say we all supported the war, probably 100 percent of us."

Dunklin was a Republican when war was declared, as he still is, but he supported Roosevelt in his decision to declare war, saying, "We all did what we had to do. My wife's brother was killed in the war. We all suffered some loss, but there was no alternative."

Once the United States was committed to the war and winning it, Dunklin didn't hear of any of his friends or classmates trying to get out of serving. Everyone wanted to go unless they were physically disabled. While some of his college friends immediately enlisted or enlisted at the end of the term, he waited until graduation. He was inducted into the army as a corporal and went to Fort Sill for two weeks, and on into officers training, receiving his commission as a second lieutenant.

"That was in 1943. After that I was trained in communications and field artillery. I finally did have overseas duty, but I had to have a leg operation, and I think that kept me from going overseas in the beginning."

He spent a lot of time in Arkansas at Camp Robinson with a new artillery battalion. Camp Robinson had been called Camp Pike during World War I, an army recruitment and training center. It was renamed for Sen. Joseph T. Robinson. "I guess it was pretty much the same, a lot of units went through when I was stationed there. You know, it's still operating, one of the camps that hasn't been shut down. It was a very active camp during World War II, and I guess it was nice being close to home, but I wanted to move on. From there I was assigned to Camp Blanding in Florida. I did finally go overseas as a replacement with the Fifty-seventh Field Artillery, Seventh Infantry. By the time I got into it, the war was winding down. But I got to be on Okinawa and in Korea and Japan. Part of my job was to round up Japanese who hadn't surrendered, [who] were still hiding out after the war had ended."

Surprisingly, almost everything about William Dunklin's wartime experiences was positive: the way he was treated, the people he met, even encounters with the enemy. After the war ended, the Japanese gave some of the soldiers small, inexpensive gifts; they didn't have much to give, but they gave mementos which many kept.

"I didn't have a hard war experience, never missed a holiday meal. Wherever I was, people invited me to their homes, just like my family did at home. I made a lot of friends, a lot of contacts, but I'll have to say I didn't develop any great skill or even any special skill."

Even the "lowest rung of society" that Dunklin met while overseas gave him a real education. He tells of one sixteen-year-old Korean who had little opportunity to advance in his life, but "he could speak Chinese, Japanese, and English" and was an excellent translator.

Dunklin stayed in the army until his release in 1946. When he returned home, his family business had three brothers working in it. "My family had a cottonseed oil mill and plant and later added a fertilizer and chemical plant. With my brothers already working in the family business, I decided I'd go to law school."

And after attending Harvard (and later the University of

Arkansas), at a time when it operated year-round with three semesters to handle enrollments, he did receive his law degree and license. However, he never practiced law.

"I married my wife, Ethel, in 1951. We had two boys and two girls and now have ten grandchildren. I have a farm outside of Dumas where I go three or four days a week. I was in real estate, too. I've done a little of everything. I haven't thought too much about the war for a long time. I'll be seventy-three in January [1995]. I don't have any horror stories. My war experiences were pretty mild. It wasn't a hard time for me."

Gene and Geneva Long

I WAS BORN IN this bedroom in 1922. When I was born, there wasn't much here, just a general store and a post office—several general stores over the past eighty years or so, I guess," Gene Long recalled. He lived in Hazel Valley with his parents for the first sixteen years of his life before moving to the small town of Durham to live with his brother, who was farming and working in the canning factory.

"I remember when the war started, I'd never been farther away from home than Fayetteville, except once, to Tulsa." Long was inducted into the army just before the war started, and Thanksgiving at Camp Robinson was his first Thanksgiving away from home. He went from there to California for his basic training, and by the following Thanksgiving, he was in England.

"I remember the train ride out to California. I stayed up the entire time. I wanted to see everything—didn't want to miss anything on my first trip across the country. I never knew our country was so big. After my basic at Riverside, we were sent into the Mojave Desert for field training. I was trained on the 90 mm and .50-caliber machine guns. I was with the First Army and was antiaircraft, a machine-gun commander. At the time, if I thought about it at all, which I probably didn't, I would have figured we'd be sent to some desert area like North Africa. I don't know how much I can tell you. I don't remember all that much anymore."

Being in the army and being in California was a culture shock for Long. "I'd never seen a colored person in my life. I'd never even seen a Mexican, and I'd never heard a foreign language."

During training the soldiers weren't told much. Then, when they landed in Scotland and went on to England, they were told even less. After what Long called "rigorous" training in loading and unloading and landing on beaches, he and his fellow servicemen still knew next to nothing about where they were going. "I didn't have any idea why we were in amphibious training. But we trained day after day in the English Channel and in the ocean. This was before D-day, but of course we'd never even heard of D-day."

He explained that the changing of dates for the D-day operation afforded them a dry run. "After the dry run, we went back to our billets, tired. But on June 6, when we actually made the landing on Omaha Beach in Normandy, the waters were so rough our group didn't make it to the beach, and we had to swim for it. There's no way to describe what was going on or what we saw. I don't know how anyone ever explains it. But there were soldiers and limbs stacked up like cordwood. I remember thinking that I could be one of them at any minute. But you don't have time to think like that for long. You're too busy. I know I wasn't thinking of killing anybody. It was just my job to shoot down enemy planes, and that's what I did."

Long miraculously made it through five major battles without a scratch, even when he crossed the Rhine and witnessed the collapse of various bridges.

"I did lose a good buddy. We had just taken out a plane. You can't begin to understand what it's like to watch someone die that way, and I can't tell you how it made [me] feel to watch a plane fall after [I'd] hit it. To be able to hit your target was doing your job, and it was a good feeling. I don't know how I would have felt if I could have seen the faces. But I don't think I ever once pointed a gun at someone and shot them—just targets, planes that were killing our men. Somehow we separated that in our mind. You had to. Can you understand?"

The antiaircraft outfits were sometimes ordered to guard a bridge twenty miles from the front lines, as they were doing when the Battle of the Bulge began. "We were right up front, and then we were forced to retreat, had to leave everything behind."

While he suffered no wounds at the enemy's hand, he did spend a month in the hospital just before the Bulge. "I was given a shot of morphine for my toothache, and he hit a nerve. It caused paralysis in my arm. I was in a hospital for about a month. I'm not sure where, but I was all right by the Battle of the Bulge."

Long was awarded a Silver Star and many ribbons, medals, and arrows, but the battles all run together in his mind now. The things he does remember, though, can still be brought sharply into focus.

"It's funny the things you remember. I remember before the Battle of the Bulge—in the forest, it was cold and the snow was deep. A friend and I went deer hunting. The deer had a hard time running in the deep snow. I remember that day as a good day, a happy day. In the middle of all that was happening, there were good memories. I remember I learned both French and German, at least enough so I could go into towns and make myself understood. Now I get my languages mixed up, but I didn't have that trouble back then."

He vividly recalled the end of the war and his trip back home by ship. "It took us fourteen days to reach the East Coast. Almost every man aboard ship was seasick. We thought we were going to die." They reached Camp Pickett, Virginia, without dying, and Long was then sent to Jefferson Barracks in Missouri for discharge.

"There were five of us from Arkansas who got together. We paid a man to bring us to Arkansas in his '42 Pontiac. I remember we each gave him twenty-two dollars. One of us went as far as Rogers, two to Springdale, one to Elm Springs, and I got off at the Fayetteville bus station. I went into the restroom, and I met this kid I knew from out in the country. He drove me to my sister's house."

Long keeps in touch with many of the men with whom he served. They have reunions about every two years. "We're more like brothers than old soldiers."

Just as Gene Long's memory began to wind down, his wife, Geneva, came in and began reminiscing: "Gene and I didn't meet until after the war. We'd both grown up here, but I was seven years younger than he was, and my family had moved to California to work in the Kaiser Shipyards when the war started. We were out there when I was in the seventh, eighth, and ninth grades. My sister was four years younger than I was. We lived next door to a farm, and I got to know the daughter who was my age. She was Japanese. We were good friends, and then they came—I didn't see them—but they moved the whole family into one of those camps someplace because they were Japanese." That was her worst memory.

She recalled that her family never suffered from any shortages. "Food was plentiful. We lived right there in the

Palo Alto–Mountain View area where there were fruit orchards and berry patches everywhere."

Many of Geneva's relatives had joined other family members in California to find work, and she looks back on those years as a family time, a good time to grow up.

"School was great. I remember at first really feeling out of place. It was so much bigger, so many more kids. And I remember the air raid drills. I remember the blackouts at night, too, but I don't remember feeling in any particular danger. The kids I knew roller-skated; we played ball, just pretty much like we always had. In 1943, I graduated from eighth grade. For the ceremony all the girls wore baby blue skirts and long-sleeved white blouses and bobby socks. We had corsages pinned to our left shoulders, and a lot of us wore flowers in our hair. Gardenias were popular at the time."

When the war ended, Geneva and her family returned to Durham. She and Gene married in 1947. They have two sons and a daughter. For a time, they returned to California, but in 1970, they came back to Hazel Valley. After years of doing a little of everything, Gene retired from his job as a tree surgeon and went back to farm life. He has photographs of his days in England during World War II before the D-day invasion and subsequent battles. When he and Geneva visited England a few years ago, he had his picture taken posing in the same spot where he was photographed in uniform during the war.

Kingston, Arkansas

G OVERNMENT RATIONING ORDERS read like a recipe for completely upsetting a way of life: Issue every citizen a book of stamps once a month, allowing them to buy limited quantities of sugar, coffee, meat, and canned goods. See that scarce staples such as eggs and butter are not used in excess, that food scraps aren't wasted, and that cooking fat is strained and re-used. Forbid hoarding, and exhort citizens to grow gardens and can the vegetables. And remind everyone that doing these things is their patriotic duty.

Perhaps these behaviors, all instituted during World War II, did change the way many urban Americans cooked. But food shortages and rationing had little effect on people in the country, especially those living in the northwest corner of Arkansas. This is an area that was marked by poverty and an independent way of life that had remained unchanged for generations.

Listening to seventy- and eighty-year-old residents of Kingston, Arkansas, is a way to get an education in self-sufficiency. In the words of many of the people interviewed, the war didn't change their lives because they'd owned very little before the war—and had little after it. Several reminisced about both their own childhoods and the years in which they raised families, and the details making up the two periods are interchangeable.

For many, the war marked the beginning of a slight improvement in their way of life, following as it did the droughts and depression ("Hoover days," as people called them) of the 1930s. Still, electricity didn't arrive in Kingston until the late 1930s and much later in the surrounding mountains, and telephones and paved roads were things of the 1950s. Even today, a number of homes in Madison County still do not have indoor plumbing and running water.

"You had to raise what you ate or you starved out," said Clercie Gibbons Bowen, who raised six children on a farm on Sweden Creek, about three miles south of Kingston. "Believe me, I canned everything I could get my hands on. Many a time I canned over a hundred quarts of green beans, a hundred quarts of blackberries, a hundred quarts of huckleberries . . . I canned vegetable soup and cabbage." Bowen preserved food in half-gallon-sized glass jars, ones she obtained by trading smaller jars with a neighbor whose family size had decreased.

She recalled drying apples and peaches in the sun, boiling them later, as needed, to rehydrate them for eating. To dry a pumpkin, she would slice it into rings, remove the seeds and pulp and tough outer skin, and hang the rings on a rod in the smokehouse or kitchen to dry thoroughly. "Then you'd take a knife and cut the rings into little chunks. It's like cooking dried apples: you boil it" to rehydrate the pumpkin, cooking until syrupy; "then you salt it off a little, put grease in a skillet, put in the pumpkin, and keep it stirred real good. We liked it fried."

Roxie Smith Cook, who also raised her two children on Sweden Creek, grew in her large garden everything the family ate, including whippoorwill peas, which were feed for stock and people, too. "And they were glad to get them," she recalled. Dried fruit, lard, and sauerkraut were stored in the smokehouse; root crops went into a cellar or hay-lined pit outdoors; sweet potatoes—which spoiled if they got damp—were covered in sand or sawdust and placed as close to the fireplace as possible, either in a cellar under the floor or in an upper story. Because white sugar was both rationed and expensive during the war, Cook cold packed fruit in glass jars (a process no longer considered safe), sweetening the fruit later when it was served.

The Cooks, and several other families in Madison County at the time, grew sorghum, which they made into molasses. And families often kept beehives or cut down trees containing wild bees to get honey. Bowen said that in February maple trees were tapped, and the sugar water was collected in buckets and used to sweeten sassafras tea. Some families cooked the sap down to make syrup or maple-sugar candy.

The scarcity of sugar during the war years was, perhaps, rural families' greatest deprivation. Cook and her daughter Charlene Grigg told a story about butchering that underscores the pain of doing without.

"We got six or seven hogs all butchered, and Grandpa went to town to get salt at the mercantile," Grigg remembered. "The man that owned it wasn't careful enough, and he loaded Grandpa a hundred-pound sack of sugar instead of salt, and nobody noticed it. They charged him for salt."

"Dad didn't notice that he was putting sugar on the meat," Cook took up the story. "He'd salt and salt and salt and rub it into the meat, and then he'd lay another ham on top—this was in the smokehouse. And when he got all through, he wiped his hand across his upper lip and tasted sugar."

"So we had to carry water and wash all that sugar off—it was all bloody," said Grigg. A return trip was made to town for salt, and the procedure was repeated. "It was just a waste, and it was rationed!" Cook exclaimed, the memory of it bothering her still. "And we hadn't had sugar for . . . ever," recalled Grigg. "If we'd had a hundred-pound sack of sugar we'd have been rich, we'd have thought."

Hogs, prior to range laws, ran loose all year, until rounded up in the fall for a final fattening on corn. Then the hogs were butchered, usually between Thanksgiving and Christmas, the meat was cured in smokehouses, and the fat was rendered into lard. Families who butchered only one or two hogs usually ran out of meat and lard before the next fall; larger families often butchered a half dozen hogs or more to keep from running out.

"Hogs sold for two to three cents per pound," recalled Dennis Eoff. He was born and raised and still lives on Bradshaw Mountain, about five miles outside of Kingston, where he and wife, Ruth, raised their five children. After the war, he sold hogs for four cents per pound, which was pretty good money for the time.

In the 1940s, most people in Madison County near Kingston hunted possum, raccoon, rabbit, and squirrel. Deer and turkey had been hunted almost to extinction and have only reappeared in the last forty years. Few people in the area kept cattle, other than milk cows, because at the time no one grew hay. Also there was no market for selling cattle, and, unlike pork, once the meat was butchered, it could not be salted and smoked; it spoiled quickly as there was neither electricity nor refrigeration.

"We ate lots of coon and possum when I was a boy," said Eoff, "and sold the skins, too. Now this was before my time, but my mother told me that way back when they didn't skin possums; they were scalded and picked like . . . a chicken. There was more meat that way." The Eoffs tried this method just once but found it was an enormous amount of work, and the meat didn't taste any different, though "the meat was pretty and white."

Bowen remembered that she would parboil a raccoon until it was tender and usually cook sweet potatoes in the same pot to flavor them. Then both meat and potatoes would be placed in a pan, seasoned with black pepper and sage, and baked until brown. "You cook them right and they're good!"

Eoff said that rabbit was always served fried and so was young squirrel. Older, tougher squirrels had to be boiled, and these were good with dumplings. "There isn't nothing better than frying up a skillet of young squirrel. You use that grease and them crumbles and make a skillet of gravy," to serve over biscuits.

Considering the amount of poultry that Arkansas provides for the nation today, it can come as a surprise to learn that rural families rarely ate eggs or chickens, though nearly everyone had a flock of hens. Bowen said that when her family ran short of money she'd gather up three or four of her heavy Dominique or Rhode Island Red hens and take them to town to sell. Eggs, which could be sold for twelve cents a dozen (Eoff remembered when they were five cents a dozen), were seldom eaten by families.

"When I was a girl living on Dry Creek, we were working in the fields one time, and an old man that lived out on the mountain stopped to talk to us," Cook remembered. "He was carrying three eggs that he was taking to town. He was needing to mail a letter—you could mail a letter for three cents."

Bread was a staple of the rural diet. While not everyone made "light" bread with yeast, all families ate biscuits and cornbread, the latter made from corn they'd grown, shelled, and taken to town to have ground into meal. According to Eoff, there was no charge for grinding; instead, the miller kept a part of the finished product, known as a toll. Cook said that the ground corn was called a "turn" of meal—supposedly because you waited your turn to have it ground.

Families grew a lot of corn, not only for meal but also for feeding stock. The leaves along the stalk provided fodder for animals. The best ears were saved to make into hominy. Eoff estimated that they grew seventy-five to a hundred bushels of corn when he was a boy, enough for a family of eight and their livestock.

A typical breakfast would include biscuits made from white flour, milk gravy, and fried pork—whatever cut the cook sliced off from a piece hanging in the smokehouse, usually bacon. Cook recalled that when company spent the night (and given the distance people had to travel by horse or on foot, guests usually stayed over) she'd kill a chicken for breakfast. "If we had fried chicken, it was for breakfast—biscuits and gravy, too, and molasses and butter."

Cook said that premium coffee beans cost twenty-five cents for two pounds, and adults drank it sparingly, just one cup with breakfast. "Kids didn't drink coffee," agreed Ruth Eoff. "I didn't drink it until I got married, at nineteen." Dennis Eoff said that he was twenty-one and in the service before he tasted any. Tea, except for sassafras and spicewood which were gathered locally and used as tonics, was unknown, and there were no coffee substitutes.

The main meal of the day was usually eaten at noon, and leftovers were placed in a warming cupboard in the oven or left on the table to have for supper. The noon meal might include side meat (Charlene Grigg called it "middling") unless a guest was present, in which case a specially saved piece of ham might be served. Potatoes, home-canned vege-tables, cornbread, and milk would make up the meal, often with a jar of home-canned fruit for dessert. As a treat, there might be a baked dessert such as an apple pie sweetened with molasses, a fruit cobbler, or a molasses cake.

"I'd make molasses cakes in big round cake pans, then layer them with applesauce," recalled Clercie Bowen. "Not under three or four layers—it took a big one to feed eight people." She held her hands a little more than twelve inches apart, indicating the height of the stacked cake.

Both before and during the war, "eating was about the same," said Bowen, "as long as we had good seasons and could raise food. You had to make out the best you could. I don't remember us ever going hungry. You'd wonder from one day to the next, though."

Dennis Eoff said that his parents wasted nothing and taught their six children to be self-sufficient. "When they thought we were old enough to take the insides out of hogs, they made us butcher. There's not a bit of difference between that and taking the insides out of a squirrel or a rabbit," something he knew how to do by age ten or so. "I squalled all the way through—but that way we knew how to do it if we had to. We were growed up tough."

Roxie Cook agreed that children were treated differently in her youth, often relegated to eating whatever food adults, who ate first, had left them. She thought it wasn't fair. Still, she wondered what today's kids would do if they had to live through times such as she has known. "I'd just like for other people to experience a little bit of what I've gone through, a little touch of what I did. I'd just like everybody to know what it is to do without, just a very short time. It'd make them appreciate what they've got now."

George S. Brewer

George S. Brewer, eighty-one, is a widower now living in Little Rock. When asked for an interview, the native of Texarkana with a background in writing sat down and wrote his own story.

MORE THAN A half century ago, FDR was sending a second round of "Greetings" to those who were barely above the sick, lame, and halt level (1-B limited service), to wit, even one-eyed future typewriter commandos like myself.

I and my gimpy-armed, sometimes limping fellow citizens were called to fill the service supply ranks of the armed services, which furnished the nearly dozen warm bodies needed to feed, shelter, clothe, and arm one man who fired the president's muskets, flew his planes, and manned his ships. May God bless them all!

The SOS (service of supply) mission was to help defeat Hitler and Hirohito and their bunch, east and west, in what was known as World War II. The mission was accomplished, but at great heart-rending cost to those who fought and to the millions who could only watch, wait, and pray.

For other ranks of this 1-B ilk, as well, the routine was dreadfully monotonous, frustrating, and boring. But there were times when army life was interesting, educational, and sometimes even downright exciting—fulfilling, too, to do one's "bit" for God and country.

As one of the lucky ones, I was assigned to my trade, newspapers and public relations. Writing for three long years for Uncle Sam was my assignment—instead of slaving for the late C. E. Palmer's chain and getting what was about the same stipend, too, considering the government gave me room, board, clothing, and cheap cigarettes. I met so many interesting people, including celebrities. I got fantastic assignments on the home front and in the European theater of operations. Then there was the bonus of getting to meet friends and fellow soldiers amongst the millions here and abroad.

For openers, while serving, I got to see President Roosevelt as he debarked from his special train to attend a 1943 Easter morning service at the main field house. Another day I squired a surly movie actor named Cary Grant around the post and met actor Melvyn Douglas before he was sequestered by a training-center general to await his commission. I also met boxing champ Sgt. Joe Louis and his companion, the great Sugar Ray Robinson, who were doing exhibition fights for the troops.

First I worked for a fellow Palmer-indentured servant, the late Lt. W. E. Hussman Sr., at Camp Robinson PRO (Public Relations Office), writing and editing the *Military News,* a camp weekly. For several weeks in 1943, the Pulitzer Prize–winning cartoonist Herblock of syndicate fame did cartoons for our *Military News.* The general, outranking us all, cabbaged the Herblock originals, but we got to keep Pvt. Jon Kennedy's offerings previously done for the old *Democrat.*

The most rewarding assignment in 1943 at Camp Robinson was showing Brig. Gen. Benjamin O. Davis of the Inspector General Department around the post during his review of troop morale. We were told General Davis was the first black general in the army's history. General Davis entered service as a buck private at the turn of the century and had been promoted through every rank. His son, Benjamin Jr., was a West Pointer and CO of the first all-black Air Corps wing in World War II.

Then it was on to the European theater of operations. My journey included Camp Reynolds, Pennsylvania (the Siberia of army camps); the shipping area of Camp Shanks, New York; and a seven-day cruise aboard the Royal Mail Ship *Aquitania*—once a queen amongst Cunard liners—to Greenock, Scotland. Then there was the Tenth Replacement Depot and a welcome transfer on detached service to supply PR headquarters in London, where I awaited permanent assignment to a continent-bound base section.

PR headquarters were at 23 Grosvenor Square, a block from General Eisenhower's castle-like enclave and across from a park (later called Roosevelt Park) in front of the American embassy. Gazing out a window, I saw a boyhood friend I'd known since 1926, Capt. Ernie Deane of Lewisville and Texarkana, now a PR type for Patton's Third Army. Imagine running into a friend among three million American troops. We "did" the city that evening, including a lovely pub that featured strong Scottish ale. En route to the tube station, or subway, we strolled through Berkeley Square, and we sang to the nightingales (in reference to a World War II tune about nightingales singing in the famous square).

I was assigned to Bristol HQ Advance Section, Communications Zone, the supply behemoth for the Twelfth Army Group organizing under Gen. Omar Bradley, who had Patton's Third Army and Hodges' First Army under him. I was billeted with a British family, Hugh and May Nenefy whose sons, Lionel and Sidney, served in the Royal

Air Force and Royal Navy, respectively. Only the daughter, Queenie, was at home at the time, and no romance ensued.

The second increment of the PR section, my group, landed on Utah Beach well after D-day, on July 14, Bastille Day, the French Fourth of July. Quivering beneath landing craft trucks, we saw fireworks aplenty, U.S. ack-ack going at the *Luftwaffe* and shrapnel raining down.

While adjusting to Normandy pup tent living, I developed a story on the Omaha Beach Command which moved supplies to the First Army attacking Saint-Lô. The twenty-four-hour ship-to-shore "duck" shuttle moved more tonnage every twenty-four hours than New York Harbor, according to Col. Kenneth Cramsie. Cramsie was another acquaintance amongst the millions. I had met him near El Dorado during the Second and Third Army maneuvers the summer of 1941 when my *El Dorado Daily News* was covering the function.

Later, I renewed my friendship with General Davis, helping set up his interview with the legendary reporter Ernie Pyle under an apple tree in Normandy.

After the bloody breakout at Saint-Lô, we went to Le Mans, passing through the flattened hamlet and experiencing for the first time the stench of a battlefield, of bodies buried in the ruins.

Le Mans was just a stopover en route east. A week after the August 25 liberation of Paris, I got a choice temporary duty assignment on the Army Group Censorship desk at the Scribe Hotel press headquarters in Paris. I logged war correspondents' copy for transmission to England and the States. After censors shredded the deathless prose, I caught hell from the writers. No matter, I had a private hotel room with a bath and clean sheets, hot water in the morning for coffee, and I got to shave for three whole weeks before turning back into a pumpkin residing in barracks in liberated Reims.

While in Paris, besides "discovering" Harry O'Neill's famed Silver Ring Bar, a one-time hangout of "Papa" Hemingway, I saw Gen. Dwight David Eisenhower; Gen. Omar Bradley; Air Chief Marshall Tedder who was deputy supreme headquarters commander; and assorted French brass officiate at the formal relighting of the eternal flame under the Arc de Triomphe, cold during four long years of Nazi occupation. The entourage was headed by the famed Republican Guard, resplendent in full armor and helmets, marching up the Champs-Elysées.

As fate or coincidence would have it, while on scribe duty, I met Capt. Ernie Deane again. I was feeding a driver from Third Army Press Camp, and he told me a Captain Deane was waiting for him outside. I also visited with the now Maj. W. E. Hussman Sr., continental publisher of *Yank* magazine. We shared a Remy Martin libation.

Lest you think I went untouched by the war, I'll tell you my luck ran out at Reims. I suffered two massive ear-drum ruptures caused by a fungus infection I picked up during the alfresco living in Normandy. I was sent to a huge army hospital in Taunton, England, where I also received additional treatment for a botched surgery I'd had at Camp Shanks. The young doctor knew what he was doing, and he almost completely cured my deafness, but when he checked my eyes, he asked, "How in the hell, sergeant, did you ever get in the army with only one eye?" Just lucky, I guess.

The Taunton hospital visit had its interesting side, waiting on trench-foot casualties from the Battle of the Bulge. A whole trainload came in just after midnight mass at the hospital. The ambulatory patient "bedpan brigade," I among them, swung into action. We had been warned that these men would lose their feet if permitted to walk. Many still lost feet despite the care and treatment they received. It wasn't my idea of fun and certainly not justice to see a ward mate hauled out for surgery, knowing his fate.

Ultimately, I went back to the continent and up to Holland. At the Rhine crossing at Wesel, I did stories on the bridge building that supplied Field Marshall Montgomery's "regrouping," two armies heading east.

Transferred back to Paris two days before V-E Day, I got to witness the biggest celebration I've ever seen. The masses gridlocked the city for a solid week while we lolled in quarters at the Cité Universitaire. From there, it was all downhill —just waiting to go home, cheered by the dropping of the bomb on Japan.

I ate Thanksgiving dinner in a tent on the sand at Camp Lucky Strike, the New York–bound shipping area for my group. But in those last days in Paris, I still kept meeting old friends. It was unbelievable. I saw Lt. George Shannon of Shreveport, Lt. Kelly Waller of Dallas, and Flem Hall, a *Fort Worth Star Telegram* correspondent. I even saw my prewar boss, C. E. Palmer. He kept asking me when I was coming back to work in El Dorado. I referred him to my current bosses, Eisenhower, Marshall, and, of course, Truman.

Coming home on the USS *LeJeune,* a converted and captured German luxury liner, I worked on the ship's daily mimeographed newspaper. I wrote a piece about the transfer of a Europe-bound soldier from a Liberty ship; he had appendicitis. Our ship had a whole medical battalion aboard.

When lining up for chow, I read a familiar El Dorado name, Lt. L. H. Southmays Jr., assistant ship's engineer. This led to yet another reunion. He showed me the innards of the ship, and the last day out of New York, he gave me the run of the ship's stores—ten cartons of Camels at four bits per, no tax on the high seas.

Another coincidence occurred as the passengers, sated with the Red Cross milk and donuts, left the *LeJeune* in New York Harbor. I carried Sgt. Fred Davis's duffel bag off the ship. Fred, from Pine Bluff, had carried my duffel bag aboard the *Aquitania* two years before when I was laid out by a botched pre-spinal anesthetic operation. Now he had a hernia. One good lift deserves another.

We were free at last with "ruptured ducks" sewn on our blouses. Christmas shopping began at the St. Louis Jefferson Barracks post exchange, a fabulous place. Then Fred and I bought tickets home and headed for the nearest bar. A touching "welcome home" occurred as we paid the tab: the bartender shoved our money back, saying, "Those guys at the end of the bar took care of it and said to have fun!" That was December 11, 1945, a merry Christmas.

One last meeting was to come. As I sat in the club car and swigged Schenley's "Black Death," along came Cpl. Emon Mahony of El Dorado, who had been in my sector at Wesel, only we hadn't even known at the time. We said our howdies and branched off at Gurdon on the El Dorado MOP [Missouri Pacific], and I went back to my lower berth, leaving a 5 A.M. call. I had to get spiffed up, you know. It seemed impossible to believe; I was back home in Texarkana after two years overseas and fourteen months at Camp Robinson.

Thus ends the saga of a one-eyed typewriter commando.

Elvin Crandell

E LVIN CRANDELL IS a retired Presbyterian minister, the man who started a police chaplaincy program in northwest Arkansas, a model program that soon spread over the entire state under his direction.

Crandell was just a "young pup" during World War II. In 1941 he was living in St. Joseph, Missouri. He enlisted in December of 1943 at the age of nineteen, choosing the Marine Corps.

"I went in with three other guys I had gone to school with. We trained at San Diego together, and we all survived the war. My memory is not what it once was, but some instances stand out clearly in my memory."

He recalled with a smile how important mail call was for the men he served with. He always received a lot of mail and packages. One of the most memorable was a Bible his mother sent to him, one he kept with him at all times during the war. "My mother always hoped I'd become a minister, and I still have that Bible. It saw a lot of action, maybe more than I did."

After his initial training in San Diego, his first assignment was MP duty, and he grew to hate it. "I know MPs are necessary. It was a pretty lively area, and a pretty active base."

Big things happened to him during the war, but not all of them on the battlefield. One of the most important events to come out of World War II was his marriage to Marjorie. "I called her in St. Jo and said, 'Come on out here and don't make plans to go back.'"

They were married in June of 1943, and his mother came out for the wedding. Elvin and Marjorie set up house-keeping in a small apartment in Escondido. "It really was a lovely little town. Those days I could hitchhike back and forth from home to the base, both ways. It was no problem. It was the main source of transportation," he said and laughed.

Crandell remained stateside until their first son, Ron, was born. But soon after, the scuttlebutt from Washington, D.C., came down: "Everyone was to go overseas." So he sent Marjorie back to St. Joseph to stay with her parents. She got a job in the hospital there, and her mother watched Ron.

Scuttlebutt also revealed his outfit was going to Pork Chop, on Iwo Jima, but that proved to be wrong. His outfit had been ready, but plans were canceled, and instead of Iwo Jima, their first stop was Hawaii. They weren't there for long, though, when they received orders to board ships for the Marshalls, for Eniwetok, and finally for "the big island, Okinawa."

Crandell recalled that it was Easter of 1945 when guns were blasting away and eighty thousand troops were on the island. "Marines, army, Marine Air Force—it was wild."

He was in the engineering division of the Marine Air Force, and much of the time he manned only a typewriter, nothing more lethal.

"Once they found out I could type, they made me clerk typist, and I typed a lot of cards, and all the time, there was a lot of 'Pistol Pete' firing as well as the constant ack-ack guns. . . . [Japanese planes] could really do some damage. It was the Fourth of July every night. There's no other way to describe it. We were told the Japanese were going to bring in their own marines, and we were ready and waiting. This one day, I heard strange sounds whirring overhead. I found out it was a plane that had been literally shot out of the sky in pieces. What we had heard were the pieces whirring by."

Mail call always brought the men back to sanity, and he looked forward to the rice-crispy treats Marjorie frequently mailed to him. At one mail call, only one name was read before the planes started firing. He still remembers that name clearly. "I'll never forget it, A-P-E-L, Apel. After that all hell broke loose."

He claimed he was a young, crazy kid with little thought of coming out of the war alive. But he was determined to have as much fun as possible, even in the worst of circumstances or in the dull routine of daily survival.

"One time I was stuck in a foxhole, or dugout, for 101 days, just me and one other guy. We decided we'd make it as comfortable as possible, and we got cots and made holes to put the legs down in the dirt, and we did get it pretty comfortable—well, as much as a foxhole can be made comfortable. And we used two-by-twos and two-by-sixes, nailing them in place. We covered the whole thing with tarps to keep out the rain. It was furnished with odds and ends, and we had it pretty well camouflaged. When under attack, that's when we'd sneak back to supplies and raid them. We'd get canned bacon, canned ham, canned potatoes, the whole shooting match. We'd each carry a case of stuff under each arm."

One night as they slept, their little home away from home was invaded by an uninvited guest. Crandell was awakened by something biting his ear. He automatically swung out at it, sending it flying onto his buddy who was awakened, just as unceremoniously, yelling about what was happening. "I told him I thought it must have been a rat. We both went back to sleep."

The Seabees construction crew was really good to the marines. "We had this buddy we could always talk out of a couple of fresh eggs. Boy, they were larrupin' good. We didn't get fresh eggs that often."

With the soldiers having an abundance of stress and anger, rotation and rest and relaxation were valued but often spent in strange ways. Crandell and a friend of his, a sergeant, would go sniper hunting or visit sites of previous battles. "We were on Sugar Loaf [Okinawa] when we came across this gravel pit that had been shelled. A young marine, hardly more than a boy, was laying there, blown to pieces."

He watched as Japanese prisoners dug at least two hundred graves each day in preparation for incoming dead carried back from front lines. Sometimes two hundred were not enough. He watched trucks carrying dead and wounded packed in like sardines.

As the war wound down, Crandell was shipped out to Japan. His bouts of malaria worsened, and he had to go to a hospital for about three weeks at a naval base on Japan. He was then assigned to occupied Japan. "Not a bad gig at all, but by that time, I had pretty well had it. I had enough points [earned for discharge] accumulated, and I wanted to go home. They tried to get me to re-up, to talk me into staying by saying they'd make me a technical sergeant [he held the rank of corporal], but in February of 1946, I headed for home."

The mainland and Golden Gate Bridge never looked so good, he recalled. He hitchhiked all the way from San Francisco to St. Joseph. Marjorie and their son were waiting.

Marjorie helped him heal from the scars of war that didn't show. She simply refused to keep reminders of the horrors and hate—she said he no longer needed them.

"She was right. When I let go of that hate, it was like a big relief. I'd long ago given it up but hadn't let go of the reminders. She was a very wise woman."

The U.S. Merchant Marine

T
HE MERCHANT MARINES were the heroes of World War II," said Robert L. Curtis of Springdale, who served on a PT boat tender during the war. And he repeated this message recently to the Ozark Mariners, a local group of veterans of the U.S. Merchant Marine, many of whom were sailing during World War II. This group of about fourteen men from all over northwest Arkansas meets on the first Tuesday of each month at the American Legion Hall in Rogers. They are the only chartered group of merchant marine veterans in Arkansas.

The merchant marine was assigned to carry cargo in support of the war effort explained veteran Robert Langley of Springdale. Merchant marine is the term applied to the collective assembly of commercial ships of a given country, and their personnel. In peacetime these ships carry passengers, general cargo, oil, and gasoline. At the outbreak of World War II, these same ships were called into service to transport troops, war materials, and fuel for the armed services.

Ed Dzalak of Rogers, founder of the Ozark Mariners, related that at the beginning of the war the merchant marine was made up of ships left over from World War I.

But soon the government began building faster ships—Liberty ships (called "ugly ducklings"), Victory ships, and T-2 tankers, all very basic—at the rate of one per day. According to printed material provided by Dzalak from the Merchant Marine Veterans National Headquarters, these new ships were assembled from prefabricated parts using a new process which reduced the time of building a vessel from a year to a few weeks. "The record time from laying the keel for a Liberty ship to its final launch was 111 hours! Over 2,700 Liberty ships were built between 1941 and 1945."

But there was no force available to man the cargo ships. "The navy was busy training its own sailors for war," Dzalak said, "so the War Shipping Administration [WSA] was formed" to oversee the merchant marine.

Dzalak went on to say that many youngsters, some as young as fifteen, eager to join the war effort, were sent to the Maritime Training Station (boot camp) at Sheepshead Bay, Brooklyn, New York. Other members of the WSA were often men classified as 4-F by the military.

In 1943 Robert Boehm of Rogers joined the merchant marine because his mother would not give permission for the sixteen-year-old to join the Marine Corps. But she OK'd the merchant marine. "She didn't know about the danger." He was a coal passer, scooping the coal into the engines of older ships. Even the more modern Liberty ships had to be oiled manually, that is, wiped down by hand. During his forty-six-year career in the merchant marine, Boehm rose to the position of chief engineer, second in command of a crew of eighty-eight men and in charge of the engine room and its crew. "You have to be in charge, have the ship ready to go, start her up," he recalled.

According to information provided by Gerry Rasmusen of Lowell, "Members of the U.S. Merchant Marine serving aboard U.S. cargo ships and tankers during World War II suffered a greater percentage of war-related deaths than did the nation's regular armed forces combined." Of 215,000 merchant marines, 6,795 died in the war, a percentage of 3.16, or one out of every thirty-two men; the Marine Corps, with 669,108 men, suffered 14,733 deaths, one out of every thirty-four men.

The United States and, consequently, the American merchant marine were neutral before Pearl Harbor, and the merchant marine was banned from transporting war goods, the national association said. Because of this neutrality, except for a few cases, the merchant marine was not attacked by Germany. However, many U.S. and commandeered Axis ships were reflagged to "countries of convenience," generally Panama, and were manned by Americans or mixed crews of many nationalities. These ships were not protected by the Neutrality Act, and because of that, suffered heavy losses, but they were not included in the numbers of losses of the American merchant marine.

Upon entering the war after the bombing of Pearl Harbor, the U.S. military understood that one of the vital components of strategy would be the establishment and operation of reliable supply lines to all fronts. This mission was assigned to the merchant marine. The American merchant marine carried out its mission as a team effort with the U.S. Navy Armed Guard. Merchant freighters and tankers were armed with cannons placed at the bow and at the stern of the ship and four antiaircraft guns along each side. Boehm explained that the Armed Guard crews manned these guns, and each merchant seaman had a gun position, serving as a backup.

At the beginning of the war, merchant ships were unarmed and were easy prey for the enemy, Dzalak's information related. Germany was well aware of the fact that the only way they could carry on a war in Europe was to sever the supply line from America. This was a fundamental part of their military strategy. A few weeks after war was declared, Germany unleashed "Operation Drumbeat," a submarine war against the supply ships. Along the East Coast the Germans were sinking American ships at will—14 during the first three weeks of the war and 373 during the next year, national headquarters reported.

Buoyed by early success, Germany embarked on a massive submarine-building program and continued attacks on shipping throughout the Atlantic, the Caribbean Sea, the Gulf of Mexico, the Mediterranean Sea, and the Indian Ocean. Over five hundred submarines were built, and hundreds were operational at a given time. A total of 833 ships and over seven thousand men were lost due to enemy action. British and Commonwealth merchant fleets also suffered great losses to Germany's U-boats before the United States entered the war. "The Germans were sinking them faster than we could build them," said Dzalak.

Americans learned a lesson of war: slow-moving ships had to be protected by a screen of fast and highly maneuverable smaller escort vessels. Radar had just been invented and was not yet refined, nor was it available for installation on merchant ships. Except for spotting a periscope, the merchant crews had no way of knowing if a submarine was lurking nearby.

The WSA and the military put the supply ships into protected convoys to cross the oceans. The convoys included anywhere from ten to a hundred ships and traveled with a protective screen of Allied destroyers, destroyer escorts, and air cover.

The American Merchant Marine Veterans related that

much of the final assembly for trans-Atlantic convoys was done in the Port of New York, the largest protected harbor in the world. On the port's peak day in 1943, during the build up for the Normandy (D-day) invasion, there were a total of 543 merchant vessels at anchor waiting for assembly. During the war, the Port of New York saw over 21,000 convoy ship clearances and 1,462 separate convoy departures, the headquarters reported.

Before the ships left the port, a convoy conference of all ship captains was held. Here they received their sealed orders, position in the convoy, planned route, pattern of zig-zag, clock, and code book for radio messages. At the appointed time and tide, the ships would pass through the submarine nets that closed the harbor entrance and head out to sea to form into the convoy pattern. The convoy's commodore ship was placed in the front row, usually headed by a navy commander who gave direct ship-to-ship orders via radio.

Distance between ships was about two to three hundred yards on all sides. These distances were critical and hard to maintain, especially in heavy seas and at night. Boehm explained that the ships sailed in black-out conditions, complete darkness, and many ships "bumped." A typical tactic was to drag a large plank about two hundred yards behind a ship so that the bow watch on the next ship could see the wake if they were creeping too close.

Al Morsani of Rogers, a World War II veteran of the merchant marine, explained that the person in charge of steering would watch the compass and travel for, say, ten minutes on a certain heading, then turn the opposite direction for ten minutes, turning in another direction for ten more minutes. This zig-zag pattern was designed to throw off the submarines as to the actual direction the convoy was traveling.

The ships on the outside of the columns were the most vulnerable to attack, but a torpedo could miss one ship and pass to one on an inner column. Escorts covered the areas around the convoy and used their detection gear to determine if submarines were in the area. When a sub was located, it would be attacked with depth charges if submerged or deck guns if surfaced.

Morsani knows well the dangers. During the war, he served on eight ships that were lost—two to land mines, four or five to torpedoes (mostly in the North Atlantic), and one to a Japanese bomber out in the Pacific. Morsani recalled that one ship was sailing the ocean by itself when a Japanese bomber flew over on its way to a mission in New Guinea. "It dropped two or three bombs and one of them hit. Usually they don't hit nothing," he told the Ozark Mariners. In another instance near the Christmas Islands, the ship Morsani was serving on was hit in the "screw" (the propeller at the back of the ship), and the ship was "dead in the water." The WSA sent a seagoing tug, three times as big as those used in harbors, to haul the boat to dry dock.

"I never once in my life saw a lifeboat launched," Morsani said, and the Mariners agreed. "It takes thirty minutes to swing the thing out. Even on the *Titanic,* they had three hours, and they still didn't get all the lifeboats launched." Instead, the sailors built life rafts of six steel fifty-five-gallon barrels with planks across. These were lashed to the ship with half–inch rope. The rope was cut, or burned if the ship was on fire, and the raft was in the water in two seconds. Each raft included a container with flares, water, dry tack, and a compass.

Morsani said that he once spent four days on a raft, and twice he was floating in a Mae West life jacket and found himself the only one around. A submarine picked him up one time, an American sub, "but I would've been glad to see even a German sub. I was luckier than a lot of them. I don't see how anybody got off a tanker. They were full of fuel and just blew up."

Langley recalled that the enemy was not the only danger at sea. "In a bad storm, cargo would break loose, and the men would have to get up at night and try to secure things banging around on the deck. The water would wash up on deck like on a submarine. It would wash anything on deck overboard. Some ships would just break up and sink in a bad storm. But the Liberty ships, Victory ships, and others built during the war were sturdier, with good engines." Langley explained that the crews tried to steer around the storms, but if they could not, it was best to sail directly into the wind. He recalled one storm when, in an empty ship in the North Atlantic, the ship steamed into the wind for twenty-four hours during a storm, and actually lost four miles.

Dzalak related that one of his boats was rammed by a whale several times; this bent the "screw" but killed the whale, which bled all over the place.

Morsani suffered other tribulations on the sea, and his mariner buddies urged him to tell his story. He began his shipping career in 1938, when he was sixteen, as a cabin boy from Hope, Arkansas, with a steamship line out of San Francisco. The ships carried over twelve hundred passengers and traveled from Frisco to Hawaii, New Zealand, and Australia. His job was to go around to the cabins, collect the shoes and shine them, and haul garbage and dump it off the stern. When the war started in 1941, Morsani got his passport and "ticket" (a WSA certification) and "a wino showed me how to tie a couple of knots." His previous shipboard experience allowed him to join the merchant marine without boot-camp training.

Morsani took his first run on a Liberty ship in 1942. "And I fed every fish in every ocean. I stayed sick until I hit the dock." This tale made the Ozark Mariners hoot with laughter. Morsani explained that the steamers were comfortable and calm, and he felt no seasickness. But on the merchant ships, he was able to eat only lemons and crackers and weighed 84 pounds at the end of the war five years later (he weighed 130 pounds going in). "One captain told me I was their worst danger. The Japanese could follow my trail anywhere." On one trip, Morsani was steering with a big bucket—that the captain didn't know about—under the wheel. The captain came in and kicked it over; this landed Morsani in the brig. The brig was in the bow of the ship near the anchor chains, where the motion of the ship was even more pronounced. And while he was in the pitch-dark brig, the anchor chains were suddenly let down with a loud noise; the scare made him even sicker.

Even though it was a volunteer position, Morsani stayed with it, needing the job. "I felt good on the beach. But if you're off the ship or you lose a ship, your pay stops." At one point he had spent twenty-two months on a ship when it was sunk. After returning to the States on an English ship, he tried to get paid, but without payroll records—which were at the bottom of the ocean—Morsani received no pay for all those months of work in a 100 percent war zone. "But I wasn't about to go look for them."

"The navy got the medals; the merchant marine got the money," said Cecil Mix of Rogers, quoting a common saying of the day. Dzalak replied that the seaman's pay was only $87.50 a month, equal to that of the navy. "The money was a big lie, but everyone believed it," he said. "We went to sea because our country needed us, not for the money." Merchant seamen received their pay at the end of a voyage in a large lump sum, but this had to see them over until the end of the next voyage.

Paul W. Dry of Bella Vista explained that the merchant seamen were not considered servicemen and, therefore, were not eligible for GI benefits such as education or home loans. Thanks to a court ruling in 1988, the merchant marine members are now considered veterans of the war and are entitled to benefits such as health care and military burials. Nor were the merchant seamen eligible for military medals, although each one who served during the war did receive the Victory Medal. The WSA issued its own medals, including a Distinguished Cross of equal merit, but merchant seamen had to pay for the military theater of operation medals. "A lot of the merchants were insulted," Dzalak recalled.

Dry said that during the war the merchant marine fleet expanded to ten times what it had been before the war. After the war, foreign shipping lines—which were able to pay crews much lower wages—took over the shipping, and the WSA laid up many ships. "That's why I quit."

Dry went to sea in 1929, working for the Dollar Line and later for Standard Oil on tankers. As the war began, many tankers were lost or sold, and many Standard Oil officers were demoted. Dry went to the WSA and was named as chief mate but, during the course of the war, was promoted to captain of a T-2 oil tanker. He was loading a tanker in Los Angeles headed for the South Pacific with airplanes on the upper deck when he received a letter relieving him of his duties as chief mate. "How can they do this?" he asked. "I know the whole tanker, can do any job possible." He was calmly told to read the last paragraph, which said that he had been named captain of a brand-new oil tanker, one that did not even have a crew yet.

He had joined the merchant marine to earn money for college, and then the depression hit. "During the depression, if you had a job you kept it." Dry said the travel and exposure he got in the merchant marine educated him. He took four trips around the world on merchant ships and visited fifty-four countries, including Pitcairn Island, home of the mutineers of the *Bounty* in the South Pacific. There he met Fred Christian, a fifth-generation descendant of mutineer Fletcher Christian, and has kept in touch with the family over the years.

Some of his ships were shot at, and half were abandoned "until we realized, for whatever reason, they weren't going to blow up. I'm glad they didn't because we were carrying 150,000 barrels of aviation gas. Once in a convoy, a kamikaze came in on the starboard, and I thought it was headed straight to me," Dry said, "but it hit the next tanker in the convoy and blew it up."

Al Morsani served on the deck crew as an ordinary seaman. His deck watch included himself and two able-bodied seamen (who had to pass a test with the WSA). The crew worked a four-hour shift, with jobs rotating every hour and twenty minutes during that shift, then had eight hours off. While on the shift, Morsani's jobs included looking for submarine periscopes from the crow's nest, steering on the helm, and making coffee for the next crew while on standby. The eight hours off were spent "in the sack" or "in the mess."

"We would carry supplies for the troops," Robert Langley remembered, "or one time we went to pick up a load of fertilizer from Chile. Munitions, food, any kind of stuff imaginable." One of his ships carried booze—his first trip for the merchant marine was a cargo ship to Honolulu carrying White Horse Scotch Whiskey for the officers' clubs there. In Hawaii they picked up navy personnel to unload ships and traveled to Iwo Jima with supplies for the troops. He served on the crew of a tanker carrying sorghum, another ship carrying bauxite from South America, and yet another loaded with sugar from Puerto Rico to fill rations for Americans on the home front. They traveled to Argentina for a load of barley and carried it to Belgium, where the people living in the war zone were going hungry.

Dzalak reported that one of the most dangerous runs a merchant ship could make was the Murmansk run, carrying food to those in the Russian war zone. These ships came under heavy fire. The fleet was losing 75 percent of the men and ships going in and 75 percent of the remaining ships coming out. Asked if he ever sailed to Murmansk, Dzalak replied, "Not me, thank God! I was a West Coast sailor, and if I found myself on the East Coast coming in, I took a train back to the West Coast." He sailed on ships in the Orient, believing that the Japanese torpedoes were less accurate. Only recently he learned that they were more exact.

Fred Umholtz of Elm Springs served on ships carrying troops home at the end of the war. He served in the merchant marine for forty-two years, 1945–1987, except for two years during the Korean War when he was drafted off the boat into the army. He has calculated that he had twenty-eight years at sea and that he spent the time on eighty-five different ships. Umholtz joined the merchant marine at age eighteen at the urging of a younger friend because he heard he could make more money in the merchant marine than in the army. While his friend was admitted immediately, Umholtz, who was just a month shy of his eighteenth birthday, had to obtain a deferment from the draft board. He picked up his application in Fayetteville, went to Kansas City for testing, and was sent to Sheepshead Bay for training.

Umholtz's first voyage for the merchant marine left New York on the last day of 1945. He was on a Victory ship carrying replacement troops to Germany and France. The ship returned with troops being sent home. Umholtz explained that the troop ships were Victory cargo ships converted for troops. About twelve hundred men were housed in the hold of the ship in bunks stacked fifteen or twenty high, two feet apart, but the men spent much of their time up on deck.

After the Armistice had been signed, Umholtz's ship carried a load of German prisoners of war back to their home. Umholtz remembered that there were several guards to watch the prisoners and that they had guns, "but I don't even know if the guns had ammunition." The German prisoners were no problem and, in fact, spent most of their time sleeping. "They were going home, and most of them knew it. There was nothing to do, no place to go, out in the middle of the ocean." Most of the Germans spoke English, and one of the German prisoners had been a bo's'n (in charge of the deck crew and deck maintenance) on a German merchant ship before capture. He asked the American crew if his men could do any work, and, although it was against the union rules, the mate put the Germans to work painting the deck right alongside the Americans, though the Germans received no pay.

Umholtz said that the German prisoners he saw had been treated well in American camps, unlike our countrymen captured overseas. "They were well fed in the States. The Germans were losing the war. They had no food for them—they didn't feed the prisoners. They were starving themselves."

Ed Dzalak explained that the merchant seamen were under the same secrecy orders as military units. "We got no news, didn't even know where we were going. Most of the time I didn't know where I was until I went ashore and asked. I sailed all over the Pacific. We did get notice though when President Roosevelt died. The whole crew cried. He'd been with us through the depression and to die in the middle of the war . . . We'd lost our captain."

Dick Hendrix

ANY HELENA RESIDENTS remember the Hendrix shoe store as a part of their lives. Its founder, O. D. Hendrix, moved to Helena in 1916 from Jacksonville, Texas. He worked for Smart Shoes for over twenty years before taking on a partner and buying the business. He later bought out his partner, renaming the store Hendrix Smart Shoes. Dick Hendrix and his wife, Bettye, are now owners of Hendrix Shoes, Inc.

"Dad retired ten years ago, but he has come into the store every day since then to greet people, until his surgery. I began working in the shoe store when I was about ten," Dick explained. "I cleaned up around the store, but I waited on customers, too. We still have one or two six-generation families who have been customers since the store first opened.

"We're only about four or five blocks over from the Mississippi River. We were really one of the lucky shoe businesses during World War II. We did a brisk business. There was a lot of logging and agriculture here back then, and there was also a camp in West Helena where they kept prisoners of war, both Germans and Italians. There was also an air training school here, and because of that, we got an extra allotment of two to three hundred extra pairs of shoes two or three times a year. The training people had to have shoes, and they'd get replaced with stamps the same as the others."

Men's dress shoes were in short supply. However, the Hendrix store was one of the lucky small-town shoe stores, having a very loyal supplier and sales representative. "So many small-town stores simply had to go out of business; the shoes went to the big department stores. See, with gas rationing, salesmen just found it easier to save gas and travel less by selling to the big stores, limiting calls. But we had an arrangement with a shoe supplier, E. E. Taylor, not around anymore, and his salesman, a Mr. Moore from Freeport, Maine. I still remember him well. We got about three or four hundred pairs a year through him."

One thing his father never did, and something he forbade anyone else in his store to do, was to sell shoes without getting a customer's shoe stamp to redeem. These stamps were coupons issued by the government to be redeemed before another pair of shoes could be ordered by the store for replacement. "He never sold one pair of shoes without a stamp, no matter how well we knew the people. We talked about other shoe stores who did sell shoes without a stamp, and I don't know how they did that. You'd finally run out of shoes. If you started with an inventory of five thousand pairs of shoes a year, you couldn't order more than five thousand pair the next year, and that's if you had the stamps. So, if you bought at our shoe store, you used your stamps." While he didn't remember specific incidents, the scenario of people coming in and pleading for shoes without stamps was repeated day after day. Some left angry, but most usually came back.

The rationing stamp programs for gasoline, coffee, meat, sugar, and other commodities in short supply were run by the government in an operation similar to welfare. Hendrix wasn't sure how the government kept records but recalled that his father spent a lot of time keeping scrupulous accounts of his own.

Hendrix was too young to enlist in WW II, but he had a brother four years older, still a teenager, who enlisted before the war ended and became a sailor. "He was really young, but he never did get sent overseas. He spent most of his time in Chicago at Great Lakes Naval Base."

Dick Hendrix and his wife, Bettye, both recalled that as children they were made aware of the war but didn't suffer much because of it. Bettye voluntarily gave up sugar but felt her sacrifice was small. "I wanted all the men overseas to have the sugar they needed. I did my part by conserving during the war. We had lots of drives at school for everything from newspapers, scrap metal, and aluminum foil to bacon grease. We saved it all and collected it. We bought savings stamps for war bonds, the whole thing."

She remembers receiving mail from overseas and how her mother would hold up a letter. It was always censored: the words were cut out so you could see through the letter. What was left sometimes made little sense. "V-mail, it was called. We never received one letter that didn't have something cut out. I guess they considered just about everything vital information."

"Young as I was back then," Dick said, "the war made a definite impression on me. People worked together more. I think we all felt drawn together in a common cause."

Nate Blumenthal

ONE OF GRAVETTE'S leading citizens is German-born Nate Blumenthal. Upon meeting him, you cannot tell by his attitude that he experienced great loss and hardship during World War II. He is a very optimistic person, seeing only positive solutions to world problems. He shows no bitterness, but neither does he attempt to cover the grim reminder of his war years, numbers tattooed on his left arm.

Blumenthal, now sixty-eight, has not forgotten what happened in Germany. He speaks freely of his youthful days spent at hard labor, of days in Auschwitz and Buchenwald concentration camps. But rather than dwelling on those times, he speaks more readily of his escape from Germany. He does not crusade to keep the memory of World War II atrocities alive, but he does share his experience when asked, the same experience shared by surviving Jews (he was Catholic), political prisoners, musicians, artists, poets, and others who became enemies of the Third Reich.

Softly he told of a happy time when he was born in Berlin, the only child of a German-born mother and English-born father. As he talked, his accent was barely discernible because of the number of years he has lived in this country.

185

His grandparents were German-born, and his family belonged to the aristocracy that was part of prewar Germany. There were parties and good times. He lacked for nothing. His father, in fact, owned the largest textile mill in Germany and traveled throughout Europe in his business. His family had "friends in high places" and believed they were "safe from the Nazi tyranny."

"No one was safe. I attended the best parochial schools available. With me, it [his political awareness] started in school in 1933. We repeated the Lord's Prayer each day. I was only about seven or eight at the time when they taught us this new prayer. It included Hitler and the Third Reich. I went home and told my father." Blumenthal was sent to live with his grandparents, who were in South Africa at the time. He was to attend school there, also. "I was allowed to return for visits, for vacations. My father still believed no one would touch us."

Conditions worsened after his exile, however, and more and more Germans feared speaking out against the Nazis. For a time, they believed their silence would save them. But by 1937 or 1938, his father was pressured by the government to convert his textile mill to military production. His father held firm, refusing to convert his mill.

"They knew they could use the cuttings for everything from uniforms to mattresses for the troops. I remember reading and hearing about the depression in the United States, but my father thought we were still in very good shape. My father traveled a lot on business, and I was still traveling freely back and forth on visits."

In 1939, during one of Blumenthal's visits home, Germany invaded Poland. And while it fought valiantly, Poland was no match for a half million men and Hermann Göring's seven thousand first-line planes ready and waiting. The Nazis used two thousand planes to bomb Poland. The Poles had only seven hundred aircraft, and most were destroyed. With no natural barriers, Poland had little defense against such strength, and the Nazis came right across the border.

It was at this time that Nate Blumenthal's father's mill was seized, his property confiscated, and both parents were arrested and separated—despite their connections "in high places" and despite the fact that his grandfather had been a German general.

"I was only about fifteen. At first, I was arrested and held in Berlin about four or five months," Blumenthal recalled. "They didn't guard me that closely, and I managed to escape and went underground with other teenagers. For the most part, we simply stole anything we could to survive. But a woman in the neighborhood called the Gestapo and turned us in. They blocked both entrances to the place [where] we were hiding out and arrested us."

The youths were sent to a labor camp at Auschwitz, a camp which became synonymous with Nazi brutality. "It was hard labor, laying railroad track, carrying railroad ties." But he was alive, and he believed the only thing that saved him was his dual citizenship, English and German. The Germans still didn't know what to do with him and were hesitant to get rid of him. But he didn't remain at the labor camp; he eventually wound up at Buchenwald, infamous for its "final solution" and for using prisoners as guinea pigs in medical experiments.

"But I was kept with political prisoners, musicians, artists, artisans, writers, aristocracy from both Germany and Austria. There was a difference in how we were treated and housed. We didn't live in wooden barracks but in brick buildings. They kept us in pretty good shape physically because they used us for trading. They would trade us for Germans they wanted released from other countries. We were just so much merchandise."

The commandant at that time took Blumenthal into his residence, "as the kid of the group. I was youngest" and best suited to walk the commandant's dogs and become his houseboy.

"I had more freedom to plan for my escape. No one actually harmed me while I was there, but I knew each day that at any time, one false move, I could be shot or traded. It was a day-to-day existence."

As the German youth began to grow taller and stronger, he volunteered to work as an electrician. The electricians were running wire to the housing being erected for the SS troops at the camp. Nate was well liked by his co-workers. With this additional freedom, his connections were able to help him slip away. A second cousin supplied him with a fake Hitler Youth Identification Card. He made his way into England where he had family he could turn to for help.

Much later, he learned that his mother had been killed in a Riga, Latvia, camp where she had been sent. His father had died in Buchenwald.

Before he and his parents had been separated, his father had given him information needed for accessing Swiss bank accounts. He made his way there and with this money helped support the Resistance. He joined with other freedom fighters and was a valuable asset. Being German-born, he could easily slip back and forth undetected across the French border into Germany and German-occupied territory.

He still smiles at those memories of working with both the English and the French. He claims it was the most satisfying time of the war for him. He felt he was contributing to world peace, and he held the hope that sanity would be restored after the war.

"It was so good to work with them, and I was involved in the fight-delaying action, or evasive action, needed to prepare for D-day."

Blumenthal was wounded several times, twice in the leg, once in the eye. He has several scars that help to prod his memory of those days.

"I think of those years as a time of tragedy, disaster for the Germans and for Germany, a disaster for the allies, for everyone, the biggest international disaster—all because of ignorance and lack of cooperation among nations. This country, the United States, was isolationist, and so much tragedy was generated, all because of fear."

Today, Nate Blumenthal has a photography studio in Gravette but is never too busy to speak out about a subject never further away than the numbers on his left arm.

Muriel Lawrence

ERVICE ORGANIZATIONS FOR men in uniform included the USO, which often established clubs near military bases across the nation. Many a young man or woman spent a little rest-and-relaxation time at a USO during leave or before shipping out overseas. The United Service Organization was not simply one program, but many coordinated under one identity, USO. One of its workers was Muriel Lawrence. A Missouri girl and a Catholic, Lawrence wanted to serve her country during World War II, and she did that by serving the men and women who defended our country. She saw that they had a home away from home in a safe, family-style environment.

"You know, a lot of people thought USO was government organized, but it was made up of a lot of groups like the Salvation Army, the YMCA, YWCA, the Jewish Welfare Board, Traveler's Aid, the Red Cross, and the organization I worked for, National Catholic Community Services [NCCS]. We all worked together so beautifully. It made no difference whether you were Catholic, Protestant, or Jew. No one even asked."

In those days, she recalled, "I was green as grass." She was only twenty-five and had led a sheltered life in Missouri. She taught physical education after college. She was still living with her parents when the war started.

"I had three days of intensive staff training to do the USO job, learn organization, stats, and finances. I worked for the women's division of NCCS. My first job was in Gainesville, Texas, the heart of the Bible Belt. I was to organize a USO [club]. There were only about seventy-eight hundred people living in the whole area, about sixty miles north of Dallas."

Being near Camp Howze with eighty thousand men was a big change for her as well as for the residents of the small Texas town. She recalls three infantry divisions from those days: the 84th Rail Splitters Division, the 86th Black Hawk Division, and the 103rd Cactus Division.

"When the Eighty-fourth pulled out to go to Europe, it was very hush-hush. But we all knew. We heard later that a lot of those boys were killed in the Battle of the Bulge."

Lawrence's main job during the war was to train volunteers for USO work. Their training was necessary in order to serve the enlisted men, "strictly privates to master sergeants. Officers had recreation facilities of their own on base. The two years I was there were the hardest work of my life."

After a more academic life, it was a shock being thrown into a life in a Texas agricultural area in the middle of the Bible Belt, an area in which she met few, if any, Catholics. But she adjusted quickly and began organizing the USO club for the hundreds and thousands of service men and women who would come through the doors.

"We were given the Masonic Lodge to use for our first canteen. At first, it was rough. Girls and women, volunteers, came in from two German farm towns in the area with their hair pinned up in curls and in tennis shoes." And this, she emphasized, was not an era when canvas shoes were acceptable street wear.

Her work was cut out for her. She began from scratch, offering classes in good grooming, walking, exercising, and sewing and even taught the girls how to talk about books and magazines so the junior hostesses would be able to carry on a conversation with the young GIs. Young wives and mothers who volunteered received classes and tips on parenting, something not common in those days.

When girls from a teachers' college in Denton volunteered to work, the whole USO operation picked up momentum. This required its move to a larger location.

"We had game rooms set up with tables, a library with newspapers from all across the country. There was always a GI interested in keeping the papers straight. We had snack bars, showed movies, had entertainment, sing-alongs, bingo games—local merchants were generous to donate prizes—teas, receptions, and a dance each Saturday night."

USO rules applied regardless of where they held the dances. At all USOs, the girls, or junior hostesses, were not permitted to leave the activities with the young men, and no one who left for the evening was permitted to return that same evening. "It was just good, clean fun."

The GIs ran the movie projectors most of the time and did any heavy moving that was needed. "If the weather was good we'd hold the dance in the park, and the GIs would help string lights and lanterns."

Lawrence recalled with nostalgia her first Christmas away from home; it was the same for many of those who came to the USO. The little Texas town helped decorate the USO that Christmas of 1942. "We were all a bunch of sad sacks at first, but the townspeople, all the merchants, and even Nieman-Marcus came through for us with so many donations." Nieman-Marcus had also sent fancy Christmas wrap, and hostesses wrapped the gifts supplied by merchants and families. A circus in the area sold locally produced souvenirs and ceramics and donated a lot of these items, which were wrapped and given to the service men and women. The soldiers helped decorate the Christmas tree. Volunteers made it as much a family celebration as possible. GIs who attended church services usually were taken home by families for Sunday and holiday dinners and treated like family.

Eventually, the Texas USO was developed to the point that it could be run almost entirely by volunteers, so Muriel went on to the regional office and then spent her time traveling three states.

"Headquartered in San Antonio, I didn't have an address. I lived out of my suitcase for the next two years and would ride the trains sitting on a suitcase—in the aisles. I traveled Texas, New Mexico, and Louisiana. Part of my job was to help young women in the service or working in defense plants and wives of soldiers and wives of defense workers."

Lawrence helped the women locate housing; there was a shortage during the war. One plant in Dumas, in the Texas panhandle, housed women in barracks, like soldiers. There were bedbugs. It went with the territory and was approached like any other problem.

"A lot of these women were away from home and sent their money home to their families. We helped them keep in touch and directed and helped them any way we could to keep up their morale."

While she was busy traveling, she didn't have time for a morale problem of her own. "I remember the day in May when the war ended in Europe. I spent V-E Day in El Paso, and several of us USO workers went over to Juárez, Mexico, to celebrate. Then on V-J Day, a group of us were in Louisiana."

After the war, she went back to Missouri and began her own self-service laundry business. "Right after the war, there weren't any washing machines. All the plants had converted to defense equipment, so it was a pretty good business. A lot of friends I'd gone to high school and college with came in to do their laundry."

Her one regret is that she threw away the scrapbooks she'd kept from World War II. She didn't think about the fiftieth anniversary year being an important, historic year.

John D. Little

I N THE POETRY inspired by two world wars, one image
recurs—that of cemeteries filled with endless rows of
graves each marking the final resting place of a soldier
killed in action. For example, John McCrae's famous World
War I poem "In Flanders Fields" opens with the image of
poppies blowing "between the crosses, row on row," and, in
the song "No Man's Land," Eric Bogle wrote that the "countless white crosses in mute witness stand."

It is the cemeteries of World War II—and the bodies
they contain—that Kingston resident John D. Little remembers and understands as well as anybody else, including the
poets. As a private with the 607th Quartermaster Grave
Registration Company, it was his assignment to process
bodies before they filled those graves. In just eleven months
and two days, the company would bury a total of seventy-
two thousand soldiers.

Little spoke at "Grandpa's," his antique shop and flea
market on the square in Kingston. "I want to make one
thing clear: I was not a hero. The guys that were heroes were
buried over there—by me. My job was to bury the dead. It
was not to kill or be killed, although sixteen men in my
company lost their lives doing this."

Little was nineteen years old in June of 1943 when the army drafted him, and he had no idea how someone with a tenth-grade education ended up in a technical outfit. Still, he had one qualification for the grisly job he would under-take: "In Kingston, where I was raised, every time there was a death in the community they'd turn school out, because everybody knew everybody. We'd all go to the cemetery and view the body. So I'd seen a lot of dead bodies before I was nineteen years old. Of course, those bodies were dressed for burial."

Following basic training in Cheyenne, Wyoming, Little's company, which included professional morticians, began specialized unit training. This involved witnessing—and occasionally assisting in—autopsies in the Denver city morgue. The men were also required to eat dinner in their seats in the morgue's amphitheater while a body was being autopsied, as part of a process to toughen up the men for their future work.

In March 1944, the company shipped out for England and, after maneuvers in Swansea and Oxford, began to pre-pare for the invasion of Normandy. Although they intended to land on June 6, the first day of the invasion, a storm caused Little's LST (landing craft) to land on Omaha Beach the morning of June 7.

"The water was the color of blood. The first body I saw, a sailor, floated by our LST before we ever unloaded. We hit the beaches by platoon, and ours hit with the Fifth Engineer Special Brigade. When we got to the beach, we had to locate our troops. Once we had map coordinates for where they'd be and where we'd be, we had to start collecting and trans-porting bodies off the beach."

The dead from the Normandy invasion were buried in the hurriedly created cemetery called Saint-Laurent-sur-Mer, which overlooks the invasion beach, near the town of Saint Laurent. (Today, it is known as the American Cemetery.) In addition to clearing the beaches of bodies, for over a week the men picked up bodies that washed ashore with every incoming tide, and they also had to cut free the bodies trapped in ships' propellers, when they were exposed at low tide.

"We had two colored companies—today we'd say 'service' companies—who were attached to us and who did all the digging of graves." Soon German prisoners of war were used to do the digging, guarded by the service companies. The POWs, who initially thought they were being made to dig their own graves and assumed that they would shortly be executed, wept as they worked. Once they saw the graves' true purpose they cheered up and were good workers.

Little's company moved on to Saint-Lô, where the first combined operation of air and ground forces took place and where there were many American deaths. He was among the troops that entered Paris following its liberation and was in Belgium during the Battle of the Bulge.

"The collecting teams of the grave registration [unit] had to be with whatever outfit was on the front. Our job was to get the dead out of the sight of new troops coming up, so the replacements didn't see them when they got up there. Most soldiers don't know what happens, because they don't expect to be killed in battle. You can think how demoralizing it would be."

It was a grisly way of life. In an era before masks or rubber gloves were used, a day's work would leave each soldier covered in blood; clothes had to be washed in gasoline to remove contamination. And the smell of decomposing bodies—especially during hot weather—was overpowering. "You get used to it, but you never forget it."

Until Congress passed an act allowing American dead to be buried on German soil, bodies were trucked, sometimes as much as four hundred miles, from the German front into Belgium for burial. Even then the regulations specified that the enemy could not be buried with the American dead. The solution, according to Little, was to run a fence the length of the cemetery and bury the Germans on the other side.

Military cemeteries were laid out in plots of two hundred graves each, ten rows with twenty graves to a row, and each grave was given a number and alphabetical designation. Any American soldier who did not die with honor (being shot for desertion, for example) was buried outside of the main plot. Henri Chapelle Cemetery in Belgium, which was used primarily for soldiers killed in the Battle of the Bulge, ultimately contained around thirty-seven thousand graves.

The Grave Registration Company buried, in Little's words, "everybody: English, Danish, French, Germans, civilians, Red Cross nurses, Americans, allies, enemies, enemy allies." An attempt was made to identify every body, which was possible because people carried identification papers at all times.

The processing procedure was as follows: As each body was identified—usually from the pair of dog tags worn around the neck—information such as wounds and tattoos was recorded, fingerprints were taken, a dental record ("tooth charting") was made, and all personal effects were removed from pockets, to be returned to the person's family. "We got pretty good at telling when a girl's picture belonged in a wallet and when it didn't, and we'd destroy any pictures we thought didn't necessarily belong there." Then the two dog tags would be separated, one placed in the corpse's mouth, the other nailed to a wooden cross. The body was then

placed inside a regular bunk-sized mattress cover, tied at
head, waist, and feet, and buried. The wooden cross marked
the head of the grave; later each was replaced with a permanent stone cross or Star of David. At intervals, chaplains
from all faiths would come and say funeral services over the
graves.

During the rush to process the enormous numbers of
dead following the Normandy invasion, bodies were picked
up and buried with whatever live ammunition (such as
grenades and mortars) they had on them; there was no
means of disposal. Later, ammunition was removed from
the dead, bulldozed into a large hole, and then covered
over—unexploded. "Today there's probably people farming
or living on top of this and don't know it. They shouldn't
dig it up, I guarantee that. I know where it's all at."

Little recalled that twice he had to bury the bodies of
boys he'd known: Norman Misenstead from Kingston and
Junior Bayles, the brother of a friend from St. Paul. "This
was during the Battle of the Bulge, and both were killed in
battle. You didn't have time to have too many feelings. We
buried them just like everyone else." But he personally went
to the grave with each one.

Little witnessed the execution of thirteen Germans
caught wearing American uniforms, his job being—once
again—to dispose of their bodies. He also helped remove
bodies from the concentration camps at Buchenwald and
Auschwitz, one of the worst things he had to do during the
war. "We took the bodies to the allied cemetery for burial," he
recalled, adding that no attempt was made at identification.
"Some of the bodies were hanging out of the incinerators;
some were stacked up on railroad cars. And then the survivors, working in the camps—they didn't look like human
beings. They weighed sixty, maybe seventy pounds."

He also saw and cleared away the aftermath of the Malmedy massacre, which took place December 17, 1944, in Belgium. One hundred and fifty American soldiers were ambushed by the Germans and taken prisoner. Suddenly, for reasons never determined, the Germans opened fire, killing eighty-five of the prisoners. The rest escaped. The bodies, dead for four weeks and completely covered with snow before being found, had frozen so quickly there was no blood in the wounds.

"This was a little more technical because we had to make note of the entrance and exit of all bullet wounds and double-identify everybody, because there was going to be a trial, and it had to stand up in court. So we had to be extra careful on them, and we treated every one like he was unidentified."

Of all of the dead from the war in Europe, very few remained unidentified—less than one percent of one percent, according to Little. Identification could be complicated by a body wearing two dog tags and having someone else's tag in its pocket, resulting in an automatic classification of unidentified until a ruling could be made back in the United States. He said that the stories about the wrong bodies being shipped back home are myths, given the care taken in identifying each body and the records kept on each grave.

Following his discharge in July 1945 after the war ended, Little was interviewed by the government as a possible witness for the Nuremberg trials, but he was never called to testify. "People in grave registration knew more about atrocities than anybody. We'd cleaned up the death camps; we had seen the results of the atrocities—the condition of the bodies."

Little, who was awarded five Bronze Stars, the French *Croix de Guerre* with palm, and numerous other awards for his service in World War II, later served in the Korean War and was the first sergeant of a military hospital in Yokohama that treated the wounded from the Vietnam War. He has kept extensive scrapbooks on his war experiences, and they include photographs of bodies being readied for burial and of living conditions during World War II. Remembering the events of World War II, Little reflected, "I was just a kid and it was something I had to do—I thought I had to. I didn't think I had a choice. It bothers me a little, even yet."

Glo Vanzant and
Pauline Irwin

GLO VANZANT AND Pauline Irwin are two retired
schoolteachers, ninety and ninety-one years old,
who both taught school during World War II, one
in Kingston and Springdale, the other in Cane Hill and
Harrison. They both live side by side today, tied together in
friendship, common interests, families, and a lifetime of
teaching school. Both claim the war affected the backwoods
and rural areas very little. Daily living remained much the
same. Chickens were raised by nearly everyone, and ration
stamps weren't needed. Most everyone grew their own food
and canned it, eliminating the need to use ration stamps for
canned goods.

Glo Vanzant was teaching school "way back in the
woods" in Kingston when the war began. She and her husband, Oral, taught school together, he as principal, science
teacher, and woodworking instructor, and she as a math,
English, and home economics teacher. They also taught any
other courses as needed.

"We were recruited for the Kingston school by the
preacher at Kingston, and we went to work for the Presbyterian National Board of Missions. The school and church
building was beautiful, of brick. There was a nurse there,

too. The school had all twelve grades, but Oral and I had the high school. We sort of split the students, about forty, down the middle. He was principal, too. Oral and I had to borrow $300 to finish our schooling in the depression, and then we went to work teaching for $40 a month. Then we moved into Springdale and tried strawberry farming for a while. That's the hardest work I've done in my whole life. Anyway, when that Kingston preacher came to ask us to teach school for $125 a month, we thought we had died and gone to heaven. We said yes."

Oral and Glo Vanzant moved to Kingston in 1933, taking their daughter, Donna, who was just three years old. They worked and stayed in Kingston for ten years.

"We loved it there. It was such a rural community of just good, honest people, poor but honest. I don't think anything changed for them, and with gas rationing, you never got into town much. It was mainly a Baptist community, and it took them a while to accept us, but they did, and we were happy there."

The mission school received a lot of outside help from the church, particularly a Presbyterian church in Philadelphia.

"They were always sending us big barrels of things, clothes, hats, evening gowns. This was a community that had hardly ever seen an evening gown, much less had any need for one. Well, we just tore them up and used the material in the gowns in home economics. They weren't wasted. They'd send other things, too, dishes and silverware. We finally started a lunchroom at the school while I was there, and I cooked for the kids. That got to be quite a chore."

Kingston didn't have electricity, and so the Vanzants didn't, either. Nor did they have running water in the beginning, though they did have a radio that ran on a battery.

Glo's daughter, Donna Charlesworth, recalled that listening to the radio was a real treat and that she was only allowed to listen to two programs, *Amos and Andy* and *Fibber McGee and Molly,* for fear the battery would run down.

When the school had running water and indoor toilets installed, a line was run to the Vanzant's yard, and Glo didn't have to carry water after that.

In 1943 the Vanzants were asked to teach at Springdale High School, and Oral became principal there. They were sad to leave their Kingston friends, but they returned to Springdale.

"Oral taught there for eighteen years. I taught there until I had Linda in 1947 and Patsy in 1948. I remember it was different at first, getting used to it after Kingston. I taught ninth-grade English; Oral started their woodworking program. That first year we were there, the kids egged our house, and I remember it was quite a rivalry between Fayetteville and Springdale, but I don't remember much about the war affecting us. We just taught school. We lived on Meadow and Thompson, and we always walked to school each day, no matter what kind of weather. We had a car during the war, but we didn't use it much."

Donna said that her parents' lives were wrapped up in teaching, but that they had also bought acreage at Spring Creek, and every summer as soon as school was over (usually April), they'd farm that land, coming back to Springdale each fall.

"We had fruit trees and strawberries. This was a big strawberry area back then. I also remember prisoners of war being brought into Springdale by truck. My girlfriend and I would see them; we were curious but a little afraid. They would be trucked in to work at the Welch's plant.

"My parents encouraged me to buy savings stamps dur-

ing the war, and I did. I never did cash in my war bonds
until just a few years ago, after we built the new Presbyterian
Church here in Springdale. Russell [her husband] told me I
should cash them in and decide what I wanted to do with
the money. I donated the money to our church to buy Bibles
in memory of my dad and in honor of my mother."

Glo Vanzant loved teaching, and her memories are of
how willing to learn the kids were. "Kids wanted to learn,
wanted to come to school. There were no discipline problems. We kept busy and kept them busy, and there was
something always going on at school."

Pauline (Clark) Irwin, a descendant of the Marrs family,
early settlers of Cane Hill, taught school in a one-room
schoolhouse in Harrison beginning in 1924. She made
sixty-five dollars a month.

"There were eight students in the eighth grade, two of
them were older than I was. There were six girls and two
boys. One of the boys would come early each day and build
a fire before school. A lot of the time he'd stay after school
and sweep up for me.

"When I married Clyde and moved to Clyde, Arkansas,
I taught at Cane Hill for seventy-five dollars a month. I
stopped teaching after James was born, until 1936. While I
was home I was very active with the home demonstration
clubs [University of Arkansas extension club programs]. I
was president of the Cane Hill club and the Washington
County club. We were always involved in some project. We
helped raise money to build the home economics dormi-
tory on the university campus."

Her husband, Clyde, had the distinction of having the
town named after him. When a name was being decided, he
was just an infant, but his family had settled the area in

1869. The postmaster turned in Clyde's name, and to everyone's surprise, the name was accepted by the post office.

Pauline Irwin went back to teaching in 1936. She went back to the University of Arkansas for courses, riding the mail truck in from Cane Hill each day. Her salary those years wasn't much, forty dollars a month.

"And that was discounted 10 percent if you didn't wait to cash your check. Some enterprising sorts would buy the checks up and wait to cash them for the full value. That was a pretty good return on their investment."

Irwin didn't recall a whole lot about the war—living in Cane Hill was different from living in an area where there were war plants, different from city living.

"I do remember the shortage of nylons. My brother worked at Montgomery Ward, and he'd tell me when a shipment came in. And I remember I couldn't afford to get my hair done, so I got my haircuts at the barbershop, and I went in to the shop over the Boston Store and got a permanent for the big sum of one dollar. That permanent was the best one I've ever had. It lasted me a whole year."

Irwin remembered it was 1942, just after the war began, when she and Clyde decided to raise tomatoes and peppers. They thought they'd be smart and get ahead of the game. They capped all their tomatoes hoping to get an early crop. "That year spring and summer came early. Everyone had an early crop, and we'd done all that work for nothing." Tomatoes sold at the farmers' markets or to the sororities and fraternities for three cents a pound, but when they sold the tomatoes to the canning factory in Cane Hill, they only got six dollars a ton. "A ton is a lot of tomatoes. Can you believe that?"

Wages for many in 1940, just before the war, averaged a dollar a day, and Irwin recalled that berry pickers got two cents a quart. With few farm tractors and little farm machinery, it meant most work was done by hand, including hay baling. Hay loaders and balers made ten cents an hour. It was no surprise, when the war offered higher paying jobs, that farms were hurting for help.

Her son started at the university in Fayetteville but went into the service in 1945. Pauline decided to move back to Harrison to take care of her aging parents and to teach school there. She taught first, second, and third grades, and returned to the university to get her degree. "But James got his degree before I did. I didn't get mine until 1955."

Bonnie Lunsford

B ONNIE LUNSFORD AND her husband, Claude, now live
in DeQueen. When asked about her life during World
War II, Lunsford said she hadn't thought much about
it. She claims the best time of her life is the present, and she
doesn't look back much. She likes being retired without having to worry about children, livestock, or making ends meet,
as she and Claude did before the war. Her life during World
War II was uninteresting, probably typical of most women
left at home with small children during the war.

"When the war started, we had a farm in Prairie Grove.
We were trying hard to get it paid off. We had two little kids,
so Claude went to work in Washington, D.C. His story, I
expect, is a lot more interesting. He didn't know it, but he
worked where they were making the atomic bomb. He took
the job because we really needed the money, and he didn't
think the army would want him with his bad ear. And at
first they didn't."

Bonnie was left with their small son and daughter to run
the farm. For months she worked the farm alone, but she
finally had to give it up and move into Fayetteville.

"We moved into an apartment on Mt. Sequoyah, and I
rented out the farm. I just couldn't do it alone with two

little kids to take care of. Life was pretty uninteresting for me. I never got out, and didn't do anything but look after the kids. I didn't even have a phone. I had our car, but I couldn't drive. When I'd go down the mountain for groceries, it was an all-day event. I'd have to carry my son. He was just two. I'd alternate, carrying him for a while, and carrying the groceries for a while. I'd have to put the groceries down and leave them to go back for them." It made the day long and tedious when she did have to go down that mountain with the kids.

One day her daughter, four or so at the time, began jumping on the bed, like kids will do, despite being told repeatedly not to. She flew off the bed and hit her head on the window latch. It bled profusely. "There we were on the mountain, no phone, and the nearest doctor more than three or four blocks down the mountain. I had to take turns carrying them both, and I was scared to death she might be hurt really bad. I finally made it to the doctor's office. He had to stitch her up, but it wasn't serious, she just lost a little hair."

This going up and down the mountain went on for months, until a minister noticed her plight. Her frequent treks, not just for groceries but to fill her coal-oil container, attracted his attention. He invited her to attend church with her children. She did, and he saw that she got a ride to and from church. He also saw to it that she got her coal oil and her groceries. "He was really a godsend."

Food was never the problem for her that it was for some. Coming from the farm, she had canned lots of jars of fruits and vegetables. Neighbors had butchered her two hogs, and she had cured several hams and canned some meat. "We probably ate better than a lot of people," she said.

"For a while, my sister-in-law moved in with us. Her

husband was in the army. During this time, we did do more things. We got involved in drives for scrap metal and collected things for the war effort. We'd take old sheets and pillow cases and roll bandages with other women. Rationing wasn't too bad since I had so many canned foods and didn't use coffee or my gas coupons; I'd give them to my brother-in-law. But I did miss being able to buy shoes. It seems I always needed shoes for one of the kids. And I do remember, I had to go without nylons for most of the duration. I did try one time when Montgomery Wards advertised they had some. But when I went, it was a madhouse. You've never seen such grabbing. They were all laid out on a table, and I wouldn't fight for them. I just turned around and left."

As the war dragged on, Claude, away working, was drafted, bad ear and all. However, this made her life a little easier because he moved her into a house in town, down off the mountain. "Life was a lot less complicated down off the mountain." And she had gas heat, no more carrying kerosene cans.

"He took basic training at Fort Jackson, South Carolina. From there, he went to Fort Leonard Wood. After he got settled in there, he did come and get us. We moved into an apartment and weren't there any time until his ear started giving him a lot of trouble. He ended up being sent to a hospital in Nebraska, and we couldn't go. I had to stay there with the kids, alone again, stranded, no phone. He wasn't well enough to write, and I didn't know what was going on."

Claude's bad ear kept him from ever having to go overseas, and the war soon ended. They went back to Fayetteville, looked for housing, and were not able to find any that would take children. Apartments were in short supply, and their Prairie Grove farm had been rented out for the year.

Still, they decided to check with their renters, hoping they could get in sooner. "When we got there, we found they'd already moved out, without notice, and found an apartment in town. We moved right in."

All's well, that ends well. They paid off the farm and began raising chickens for area poultry companies and the Campbell's Soup Company. They raised chickens for over thirty years. "We also had another child after the war."

Luther D. Fletcher

APT. LUTHER D. FLETCHER stood on the top deck and looked out on New York Harbor. In the dusk, he saw the Statue of Liberty, the Empire State Building, and the silhouettes of warships. Looking down, Fletcher saw men walking up the gangplank, boarding. It was the evening of June 30, 1944, and before the next dawn, the USS *Barry* would chug into the night, leading a convoy across the Atlantic and carrying Fletcher into war.

For Fletcher, an army chaplain, his last night in New York was a time to steel himself against the trials ahead. Lying in his bunk below decks, waiting for the ship to get under way, he thought of loneliness, fear, death, and dying. Fletcher wrote in his diary, "There will be bullets and bursting shells, men filled with fear coming for counsel. I too will be filled with fear. But I cannot reveal it, for I must help the others hold their courage. There will be hours of poignant homesickness and bitter loneliness. I too will be lonely at times. But I cannot reveal it, for I must bring cheer to the lonely. . . . There will be open wounds and mental disorders. I must keep courage and an understanding of mankind."

Fletcher contemplated the future far into the night, and then he felt the engines throb and the ship quiver. The USS

Barry was departing. When Fletcher arose the next morning and walked up on deck, New York had disappeared. All he could see was a convoy of ships riding a vast expanse of water.

Two weeks later, the ship landed at Glasgow, Scotland, and two weeks after that, Fletcher crossed the English Channel and landed on Utah Beach in Normandy. Over the next year, he pushed through Europe in the great Allied invasion. With Gen. George S. Patton's men, he crossed France, Belgium, Luxembourg, Holland, Germany, Czechoslovakia, and Austria. Fletcher wrote in his diary what he saw: he wrote reports, notes, essays, and homilies, and he wrote prayers. Fletcher did see bullets and bursting shells, and he certainly saw loneliness, fear, death, and dying.

At the foot of the Austrian Alps, he saw soldiers fishing in snow-melt streams. "Some of the men are using hand grenades, a most effective manner to obtain fish." From the banks of the Rhine, he saw American infantrymen ripped apart by machine-gun bullets as they tried to steal across the river, quietly paddling rubber rafts under cover of darkness. Scouts had failed to discover a gun emplacement on an island in midstream. He described the scene in his diary: "When the rafts reached the island and were passing—all hell broke loose at one time. An enemy machine-gun nest opened up on the island, enemy flares filled the sky, and 20 mm ack-ack guns opened up at point-blank range above the water's surface. Our men were caught like ducks on a pond."

Eighty years old now, Col. Luther D. Fletcher cuts a trim, distinguished figure. He is tall and angular; his features are sharp and his eyes sharper. Wearing a red cardigan, a white oxford shirt, and charcoal slacks one morning, he looked dapper and far younger than his years. But he took small

213

careful steps as he followed his wife, Nora, down the hall of the care center in Bella Vista. The colonel's memory has faded. Nora had to remind him to keep him on the topic. After all these years, a few details have escaped the colonel—whose valor earned him a Bronze Star, among other decorations—but history lives in his diary.

Sitting on a couch in the reception room of the care center, just down the hill from the Fletcher residence, Nora Fletcher carefully unwrapped the diary and passed it across the coffee table. Bound in brown leather, the book bears the title, "Blood, Sweat, Mud and Tears." In the lower right-hand corner are embossed the words, "By L. Dudley Fletcher, Captain, U.S. Army."

Along with the diary, Mrs. Fletcher passed across the table a small packet of photographs. In pencil, she had printed on the packet "Concentration Camps." Inside were images of absolute, enraging horror. Studying one sepia photograph from his position on the sofa, Colonel Fletcher said quietly, "It was to me just unbelievable. It was there. It was there, all right."

Conducting church services in the throes of a world war is no everyday business, and as Patton's men hacked their way through Europe, driving toward the core of Germany, Chaplain Fletcher delivered his sermons from many unlikely pulpits. Wherever he found a congregation, Fletcher posted his chaplain's flag and contrived a church.

On Christmas Eve, 1944, he preached while standing in front of a large mirror mounted over a marble fireplace in the German mansion of Franz Von Poppin. Von Poppin was ambassador to the United States. Fletcher stood beside the ambassador's baby grand piano as he delivered the message. "Our glorious march," he told the men, "from the Normandy beach across France to where we now stand, before the Siegfried Line, with the wreckage of the German army behind us, should convince the most skeptical soldier that God has ridden with our banner."

On Christmas Day, 1944, he conducted one of his services in a barroom in the Moselle Valley, France. Fletcher delivered the message from atop the bar. On a Sunday earlier in the winter, the chaplain held a service, "more of a devotion" than a service, in a coal bin. The bin lay within a pillbox fortification of the Maginot Line. Fletcher delivered his first sermon on German soil in Pearl, Germany; he preached in a cement factory. Conditions were often less than optimal. "The Germans were throwing in the eighty-eights—those whistlin' minnies were really coming in. I just was finishing the last hymn when they started placing them in the backyard."

During his year in the war, the chaplain conducted as many as seven services a day, wherever he could—in barns, cafes, tunnels, mansions, fields, forests, dance halls, theaters, gymnasiums, first-aid stations, hotel lobbies, schools, courthouses, cemeteries, and airplane factories. He held services on river banks, under railroad bridges, and amid the rubble of bombed-out houses. And once, on Easter, at Alsfeld, Germany, the chaplain even preached in a church.

To judge by the notes in his diary, the services always inspired Fletcher. Forever doubtful that his meetings would draw much notice from the weary, battle-hardened soldiers, the chaplain was continually amazed at the crowds. In rain and snow one Sunday, Fletcher arranged a service for an engineering battalion that had worked through the night building a bridge. The men had been told that the Germans had just bombed their bridge into oblivion, and Fletcher found the group tired and disheartened. He was certain that few if any of the men would care to attend his service, which he held in an open woods, but the men crawled from their pup tents and came. The chaplain left buoyant.

The duties of the wartime chaplain extended far beyond just leading services and put the enterprise of carrying religion into war in perspective. On Easter Sunday, before his evening services at Alsfeld, Fletcher followed his troops as they pursued the enemy. "My units were scattered far and wide—it was a strange way to spend Easter." On Wednesday of Holy Week, he and the troops were assaulting the Rhine. "The sky was overcast, and the stars and moon, a fighter's dearest friends, were hidden from view. Amidst intermittent rainfall and the heavy smoke screen shrouding the river, our men were silhouetted time and again by the lightning-like flashes of artillery, or a rocket flare. . . ." Between services, Fletcher fished bodies from rivers, he searched for the dead in forests and fields, and he helped bury them. He gave last rites, consoled the dying, and wrote letters of condolence to next of kin.

Writing his condolences one night, Fletcher discovered in the personal effects of a dead soldier a blood-soaked letter the soldier had written home just three hours before he died. The chaplain sat in his tent and read the soldier's letter. Rain drummed on the canvas, lightning flashed outside, and artillery shells exploded in the dark. "The enemy is throwing everything he has at us tonight." The candle at the chaplain's table flickered. The soldier was a good friend, and Fletcher was so moved by his last letter that he copied it into his diary:

December 14, 1944
Somewhere
Darling Sweetheart:

Have a few minutes to spare so am using them up by dropping you and our son a few lines. Just want you to know I am still all right and still have my fingers crossed. Sure hope all this ends soon. Am beginning to get the willies.

Haven't heard from you sweetheart in nearly a week. I am blaming the holiday season for holding up our mail. Am trying awfully hard to keep myself from thinking you are sick. Every time I don't hear from you I imagine all sorts of terrible things happening to you, so if you want to do something to help keep me from worrying, just write lots of letters.

I suppose you have had our son's birthday party all planned out? It just doesn't seem possible he is four years old. To think of losing my baby into a big boy surely hurts me. I would have liked so much to have watched him grow up. But I just have to keep myself from getting bitter over it. It hurts to beat hell, tho.

What are you planning for Christmas? What did you buy for yourself and for our son from me? I am sending you a package just as soon as the opportunity presents itself.

I have what I want to send you, but no way of sending it. I've accumulated quite a few souvenirs and guess I had better send them home before something happens so I can't send them.

Darling can't you write me more letters. V-mail is fine but I can read between the lines more easily in a long letter than I can a short one. And that is the only way I can find out how you are feeling about everything. You won't tell me.

Also if you have a spare cookie, stick of gum, chocolate bar, or box of chocolates, or an old nasty fruit cake laying around just throw them all together in a flour sack and send them over. I would really appreciate it up here on the front lines.

Enuf foolishness dearest. It is 2:30 in the morning and I'm so tired I am getting silly. Sure wish these damned guns would stop for just 30 minutes so I could rest. Tell our baby that daddie will write him a birthday letter. I love you snookums with all my heart. I love you and our baby forever.

Yours . . .

Some revisionists now dispute the accounts of the atrocities that the Nazis committed during the war. They contend that the crimes, torture, and mass extermination have been exaggerated, or even that they never occurred. Some call the holocaust a hoax. Even during the war, Fletcher was familiar with the cynic's view of the horrors. "Germans you meet scoff unbelievingly when you tell them about atrocities committed in their midst and in their name." But he toured the death camps in Germany and Austria. He saw the atrocities and wrote vivid descriptions of what he discovered in the camps. He toured Dachau, Germany, and Lambach, Austria, but the fullest account written in his diary was of Buchenwald, near Weimar, Germany. The Allied troops led German civilians on a tour of the camp to ensure that they knew the enormity of the crimes committed. A people who knew the evils that occurred in the camps would never allow them to happen again.

The report on Buchenwald that Fletcher wrote in his diary contains unflinching descriptions of the unmitigated horrors he saw there:

> One thousand Weimar citizens toured the Buchenwald camp in groups of 100. They saw blackened skeletons and skulls in the ovens of the crematorium. In the yard outside, they saw a heap of white human ashes and bones.
>
> They saw a hospital that no one would dare call a barn. Four tiers of boards up to the ceiling on either side of a wide aisle, now and then a filthy German blanket, but mostly a few croker bags on the hard planks among filth and disease. Men were dying like flies—dying at the rate of 500 per day. While I was there many died. A slight noise and they were dead, some not strong enough to even utter a noise. Dead from malnutrition, only that's too beautiful a word—let's call it starvation.
>
> The living actually looked worse than the dead. Those

who lived wore striped uniforms, with the stripes running up and down. Those who were dead were stripped of their clothing and lay naked, many stacked liked cordwood waiting to be burned in the crematory. At one time, 5,000 had been stacked on the vacant lot next to the crematory.

The guide, a young Polish lad who spoke excellent English, took me through the place and explained what took place step by step. He knew, for he had been there five years. To kill a man, they gave him a bath and stripped off his clothing, then sent him down a narrow corridor. There he was hit in the head with a large potato masher— a long wooden stick like a baseball bat. When he dropped, he was cut open with a knife by the surgeon who stood by with a washbowl, rubber apron and gloves. Over the wash- bowl was the sign "Cleanliness is important here."

The procedure reminded me of stockyards of Fort Worth, Texas. The surgeon removed all gold from the teeth of the dead man. Then he was stacked like cord wood on the lot adjacent to the crematory. They were burning them at the rate of 400 per night.

At headquarters of the SS troops who ran the place were lamp shades made from human skin taken from the chest of a man while they tortured him alive.

We were told that they had taken all the cultured and educated people of the conquered countries who opposed them and placed them here to die of hard work and star- vation.

At Buchenwald, there was formerly a large buzz- bomb factory. The two huge wings of the factory were connected in the middle by a large mess hall that fed the workers of both wings. Here I saw one of the finest jobs of bombing to the pinpoint I have ever witnessed—a great tribute to the Air Force. They destroyed completely both wings of the factory and left the mess hall standing. Five hundred people died in the factory bombing because the SS locked the doors and would not let them out.

Often, the guide said, the SS wished to make an example of someone in killing him. They hung him on the lot adjacent to the crematory, and all the three sections of the camp witnessed the sight—some 30,000 prisoners. They used what I call hay hooks, catching him under the chin and the other in the back of his neck. He hung in this manner until he died. The guide said he had witnessed men hanging five hours before dying. I also saw board walls called torturing racks with sharp hooks on which a man was hung and left to die. The walls bore the marking of where they had scratched and clawed in their dying hours.

Fletcher saw much more during his year in the war. He interviewed political prisoners; he wrote scathing diatribes against the Nazi's philosophy of religion and the Nazi's ethics; he complained mightily about "Who me? Germans." He saw them as duplicitous, knowing more about the activities of the Nazis than they let on.

In all, his diary fills about 150 typed pages. It shows him to be a keen observer, and fifty years later, the wish is that he'd written 150 more pages.

At an August service at war's end in 1945, he began:

We are assembled here this morning, a day that will go down in history, the first day of peace on earth in 14 years. We would not forget this morning, that this day was bought with a price. We have measured this price not in terms of guns, tanks, planes and ships, but in terms of 260,000 comrades who now sleep beneath the whitened crosses that stretch from Utah Beach in Normandy to the islands of the Pacific.

This small group, and the other small groups that go to make our mighty allied armies around the world, representing men of all faiths and creeds, all colors and nationalities, have fought with oneness of spirit and a unity of purpose that has made this day of peace possible. And it is with this same spirit and unity that we shall give to the world freedom from want, freedom from fear, freedom of worship, freedom of speech and freedom of the press, thus making it a better world in which to live.

It is the individuals as yourselves working together as a team, undergoing hardships without complaint, suffering privations, making sacrifices, making this day of peace on earth possible.

I take this opportunity to thank you personally for that spirit, courage and faith. And wish for you all a speedy trip home and quick readjustment to normal living. May we not forget our pledge to our comrades departed to make this day of peace a lasting peace on earth, and good will among men.

Contributors

GEORGE S. BREWER is a widower now living in Little Rock, Arkansas. When asked for an interview, the native of Texarkana with a background in writing sat down and wrote his own story and the story about John J. "Joe" Leroux.

After the war Brewer was city editor of the *Eldorado Daily News*. From 1957 to 1970 he was in public relations, and from 1970 to 1981 he worked for the State Chamber of Commerce.

ABBY BURNETT has worked as a freelance writer since 1990. Her articles have appeared in magazines based in the Midwest, and she has written feature and news articles for a variety of newspapers in northwest Arkansas. Burnett also covers events in Madison County for the *Morning News of Northwest Arkansas*. In addition, she writes a weekly food column for the *Morning News* entitled "The Back Burner," which combines backgrounds on food, readers' requests for recipes and information, and general culinary observations.

KAY B. HALL is a reporter and feature writer for the *Morning News of Northwest Arkansas*. She has won numerous awards for her journalism and has edited the first volume of the four-volume *Orphan Train Riders: Their Own Stories* (1992–ongoing, Orphan Train Heritage Society of America).

LAURINDA JOENKS of Springdale, a 1988 journalism graduate of the University of Arkansas, is the special-sections editor at the *Morning News of Northwest Arkansas*. She has been on the staff for five years and has also held the position of wire editor. Prior to her employment at the Springdale paper, Joenks was a copy editor/reporter at the *El Dorado News Times*. She was awarded the first-place feature award from the Arkansas Press Association in 1988 and has won other awards for headline writing, page design, and coverage of tourism.

MARY ELLEN JOHNSON was a publisher's assistant on the Washington County History Book project sponsored by Shiloh Museum, from 1986 until 1989. During this time, and following the conclusion of the project, she wrote a weekly column for the *Northwest Arkansas Times*.

In 1986, Johnson founded the Orphan Train Heritage Society of America, preserving the history of an era in America's history from 1854 until 1929 when over 150,000 orphaned, abandoned, or homeless children were "placed out." Part of her responsibilities include compiling and editing a quarterly newsletter, "Crossroads," and she is currently putting together the fourth book in the *Orphan Train Riders* series.

MARK MINTON works as a reporter for the *Morning News of Northwest Arkansas*, where he is responsible for covering a wide range of topics: transportation, education, criminal justice, municipal, and other issues.

Minton is a 1989 graduate of the University of Arkansas,

where he earned a bachelor's degree in journalism. After graduation, he worked as a reporter for the *Pine Bluff Commercial* for about two years before moving to northwest Arkansas and joining the *Morning News*. He now lives and works in Springdale.

HEIDI STAMBUCK is a Newton County native who worked as a reporter for the *Log Cabin Democrat* in Conway and the *Morning News* in Springdale, Arkansas, before quitting to stay home with her son, Zachary.